Quick & Easy
Wedding Cakes

Quick & Easy
Wedding Cakes

KAREN GOBLE

NEW HOLLAND

DEDICATION

To all my family and many friends that, as always, encouraged and supported me during the making of this book. Thanks for not minding the latenight phone calls when I thought the computer had eaten all my instructions and I was in a mad panic!

First published in 2006 by New Holland Publishers (UK) Ltd
London • Cape Town • Sydney • Auckland

Garfield House, 86–88 Edgware Road, London, W2 2EA, United Kingdom
www.newhollandpublishers.com

80 McKenzie Street, Cape Town 8001, South Africa

14 Aquatic Drive, Frenchs Forest, NSW 2086, Australia

218 Lake Road, Northcote, Auckland, New Zealand

ISBN 13: 978-1-84537-413-6
ISBN 10: 1-84537-413-4

Senior Editor: Clare Hubbard
Editorial Direction: Rosemary Wilkinson
Design: Gülen Shevki-Taylor
Photographer: Shona Wood
Production: Hazel Kirkman

1 3 5 7 9 10 8 6 4 2

Reproduction by Pica Digital PTE Ltd, Singapore
Printed and bound by Times Offset, Malaysia

Note

The author and publishers have made every effort to ensure that all instructions given in this book are safe and accurate, but they cannot accept liability for any resulting injury or loss or damage to either property or person, whether direct or consequential and howsoever arising.

Because of the slight risk of salmonella, raw eggs should not be served to the very young, the ill or elderly, or to pregnant women.

In the recipes use either metric or imperial measurements, but never a combination of the two, as exact conversions are not always possible.

Acknowledgements

Renshaw Scott Ltd for supplying the Regalice sugarpaste (rolled fondant) for all the cakes in this book; Culpitt Limited for tools and equipment; Pat Trunkfield at PME for her help and support with equipment; Keith Smith of Major Johnson for supplying unusual shaped cake dummies and boards; Marion Frost of Patchwork Cutters Ltd. Very special thanks to my best friend, Lesley Tanner, for the use of her studio and last but not least Yvonne Berns for encouraging me to do the first book.

Contents

Introduction

Most family celebrations feature a cake of some sort, but at a wedding the cake forms a focal part of the day – "the bride and groom are now going to cut the cake." People always want a photograph of this moment, so it's important that the cake looks stunning. However, this doesn't have to mean a big, elaborate creation. A simple, classic design can look just as beautiful.

Although I am well-known in the sugarcraft world for making sugar flowers and modelling, I thought it was time to show a very easy approach to making simple but stunning cakes. Most of the cakes use ready-made products, which can be purchased from your local suppliers. This book contains 22 cake designs. There is a wide variety of styles, shapes and sizes, from the traditional to the very flamboyant, so there will definitely be something for you whatever the style and theme of wedding.

You can easily adapt the designs to suit your own requirements by changing the colours and decoration, and many of the designs could be adapted for other occasions such as anniversaries and birthdays. I do hope this book will spark your imagination and that you enjoy making your own wedding cake.

Regal Elegance (pages 94–97).

Equipment

Here is a list of the tools and equipment that I used when making the cakes in this book. Many of the items are part of the basic "kit" that any cake decorator needs, others you will only use now and again. Get to know your gadgets, as many of them can be used in a variety of ways.

Acetate Useful when making royal icing runouts. Can also be used for stencils.

Bowls You will need a variety of bowls for mixing cake mixture, icings etc.

Cake boards Come in a wide variety of shapes and sizes, generally silver or gold in colour.

Cake leveller Used to level the top of the cake and also to split the cake horizontally.

Cake tins (pans) Have an assortment to hand.

Clingfilm (plastic wrap) Use to cover pastes and icings as it stops them from drying out and keeps them fresh.

Cocktail sticks Use to add colour to icing.

Crimpers Use to create a pattern in sugarpaste (rolled fondant) on cakes and boards. Various types available.

Cutters A vast range of shapes is available in both plastic and metal – stars, flowers, hearts etc.

Dusting powders Mainly used to colour sugar flowers.

Electric mixer Essential piece of time-saving equipment.

Embossers Create a pattern in sugarpaste (rolled fondant) – can be used to great effect on cakes and boards.

Greaseproof (waxed) paper Essential for the cake maker and decorator. Used for wrapping cakes, lining tins (pans) and making piping (decorating) bags and templates.

Moulds Come in all shapes and sizes, useful for modelling.

Non-stick mat Useful when assembling small elements – flowers/models etc. as paste slides off mat easily.

Paintbrushes Used for painting and adding delicate details. Also used for applying dusting powders.

Palette knife An absolute must-have. Useful for spreading, mixing and lifting.

Paste colours These are more concentrated than liquid colours and do not make your icings/pastes sticky.

Piping (decorating) bags Greaseproof paper, reusable and disposable piping bags are available.

Piping tubes (nozzles) These come in all shapes and sizes and are used for piping.

Rolling pins Come in all sizes. Use a large one for rolling out big pieces of sugarpaste (rolled fondant) for covering cakes and boards and a small one for flowers, modelling etc. I would recommend using non-stick.

Scissors Make sure they are sharp – used for making piping (decorating) bags, cutting linings for tins (pans) etc.

Sharp knife Another must-have item. Useful for trimming sugarpaste (rolled fondant) from around boards.

Smoother Eliminates lumps and bumps from sugarpaste (rolled fondant) and marzipan to give the cake a professional finish.

Spirit (carpenter's) level To start with, use to check that your oven is level. Mainly used for checking that cakes are level.

Sugarcraft (rolled fondant) tools There are so many tools on the market today – they are very useful for modelling. You can often use the same tool to create different effects.

Tape I mainly use two sorts of tape: paper floristry tape for binding flowers and sprays and double-sided tape to attach ribbon around cake boards.

Tape measure/ruler You will use this all the time.

Textured rollers There are many patterns available and they give a fantastic effect when used on sugarpaste (rolled fondant).

Turntable There are many different turntables on the market but I find one that can tilt is most useful as it makes it easier when working on the side of the cake.

Tweezers Both straight and angled tweezers are available.

Veiners Enable you to get a realistic effect on leaves and petals.

Veining board When paste is rolled over board a vein is created into which wire can be inserted.

Wires The thickness of wire is referred to as the gauge. The higher the gauge the finer the wire.

The Cake Itself

Is it going to be a madeira, chocolate or fruit cake? What type of filling and covering is appropriate? How many people does it need to serve? This section will help you make the right choices.

Cake Sizes and Portions

The tables below detail the approximate number of slices you can get from cakes of various sizes.

Sponge Cake

SQUARE

CAKE SIZE	13cm (5in)	15cm (6in)	18cm (7in)	20cm (8in)	23cm (9in)	25cm (10in)	28cm (11in)	30cm (12in)
PORTIONS	12	18	24	32	40	50	60	72

SHAPED

CAKE SIZE	13cm (5in)	15cm (6in)	18cm (7in)	20cm (8in)	23cm (9in)	25cm (10in)	28cm (11in)	30cm (12in)
PORTIONS	10	14	20	25	33	39	49	56

Sponge cakes are usually cut into slices measuring approximately 2.5 x 5cm (1 x 2in).

Fruit Cake

SQUARE

CAKE SIZE	13cm (5in)	15cm (6in)	18cm (7in)	20cm (8in)	23cm (9in)	25cm (10in)	28cm (11in)	30cm (12in)	
PORTIONS	27	36	51	64	84	100	125	144	

SHAPED

CAKE SIZE	13cm (5in)	15cm (6in)	18cm (7in)	20cm (8in)	23cm (9in)	25cm (10in)	28cm (11in)	30cm (12in)	
PORTIONS	21	28	40	50	66	78	98	113	

Fruit cakes are usually cut into slices measuring 2.5 x 2.5cm (1 x 1in).

Apricot glaze/Marzipan/Sugarpaste (Rolled fondant)

This table shows you how much apricot glaze, marzipan and sugarpaste are needed for cakes of various sizes.

CAKE SIZE

SQUARE TIN	13cm (5in)	15cm (6in)	18cm (7in)	20cm (8in)	23cm (9in)	25cm (10in)	28cm (11in)
ROUND TIN	15cm (6in)	18cm (7in)	20cm (8in)	23cm (9in)	25cm (10in)	28cm (11in)	30cm (12in)
Apricot glaze	15ml (1 Tbsp)	22ml (1½ Tbsp)	30ml (2 Tbsp)	37ml (2½ Tbsp)	45ml (3 Tbsp)	45ml (3 Tbsp)	60ml (4 Tbsp)
Marzipan	375g (12oz)	750g (1½lb)	875g (1¾lb)	1kg (2lb)	1.25kg (2½lb)	1.5kg (3lb)	1.75kg (3½lb)
Sugarpaste	500g (1lb)	750g (1½lb)	875g (1¾lb)	1kg (2lb)	1.25kg (2½lb)	1.5kg (3lb)	1.75kg (3½lb)

Cake Recipes

Light Fruit Cake
This is a moist cake with a delicious flavour. The key ingredient is the succulent apricots. (c = cup/st = stick)

SHAPED TIN	15cm (6in)	18cm (7in)	20cm (8in)	22cm (9in)	25cm (10in)	28cm (11in)	30cm (12in)	
SQUARE TIN	12cm (5in)	15cm (6in)	18cm (7in)	20cm (8in)	22cm (9in)	25cm (10in)	28cm (11in)	30cm (12in)
Mixed dried fruit	250g (9oz/ 1½ c)	440g (15½oz/ 3 c)	500g (1lb 2oz/ 3½ c)	750g (1lb 9oz/ 4½ c)	1kg (2lb 4oz/ 6¾ c)	1.25kg (2lb 12oz/ 8¼ c)	1.5kg (3lb 4oz/ 9¾ c)	1.75kg (4lb/ 12 c)
Mixed peel	15g (½oz/1 Tbsp)	30g (1¼oz/¼ c)	30g (1¼oz/¼ c)	60g (2¼oz/½ c)	90g (3¼oz/½ c)	125g (4¼oz/¾ c)	140g (4¾oz/¾ c)	150g (5oz/1 c)
Chopped dried apricots	60g (2¼oz/½ c)	60g (2¼oz/½ c)	125g (4¼oz/¾ c)	185g (6½oz/1 c)	250g (9oz/1½ c)	315g (11¼oz/2 c)	370g (13oz/2½ c)	435g (15½oz/3 c)
Brandy	40ml (1½fl oz/ 2 Tbsp)	40ml (1½fl oz/ 2 Tbsp)	40ml (1½fl oz/ 2 Tbsp)	60ml (2fl oz/ ¼ c)	60ml (2fl oz/ ¼ c)	80ml (2¾fl oz/ ⅓ c)	120ml (4fl oz/ ½ c)	160ml (5fl oz/ ⅔ c)
Softened butter	160g (5¼oz/ 1½ st)	250g (8¾oz/ 2 st)	315g (11¼oz/ 3 st)	440g (15½oz/ 4 st)	525g (1lb 3oz/ 4¾ st)	625g (1lb 6oz/ 5½ st)	880g (1lb 15oz/ 7¼ st)	1kg (2lb 4oz/ 9 st)
Light brown sugar	160g (5¼oz/ 1 c)	250g (8¾oz/ 1½ c)	315g (11¼oz/ 2¼ c)	440g (15½oz/ 3 c)	525g (1lb 3oz/ 3¾ c)	625g (1lb 6oz/ 4 c)	880g (1lb 15oz/ 6 c)	1kg (2lb 4oz/ 7 c)
Medium eggs	2	4	4	5	6	7	10	11
Plain flour (all-purpose)	185g (6½oz/ 1½ c)	315g (11¼oz/ 2¾ c)	375g (13oz/ 3¼ c)	500g (1lb 2oz/ 4½ c)	625g (1lb 6oz/ 5½ c)	750g (1lb 10oz/ 6½ c)	1kg (2lb 4oz/ 9 c)	1.2kg (2lb 12oz/ 12 c)
Ground mixed spice (pumpkin pie spice)	1 tsp	1½ tsp	2 tsp	3 tsp	4 tsp	5 tsp	6 tsp	7 tsp
BAKING TIME	2 hrs 5 mins	2–2¼ hrs	3–3½ hrs	3½–3¾ hrs	4 hrs	4½–4¾ hrs	5–5½ hrs	5¼-5½ hrs

1 Mix together the fruit, peel, apricots and brandy. Cover. Leave for several hours until the liquid has been absorbed.
2 Preheat the oven to 140°C/275°F/Gas mark 1. Lightly grease the tin and line the base and sides with baking parchment or greaseproof paper.
3 Beat the butter and sugar until well combined. Gradually add the eggs, beating well after each addition.
4 Transfer to a large bowl and stir in the sifted flour and spice. Stir in the soaked fruit.

5 Spoon the mixture into the tin and smooth the surface. Gently tap the tin to remove any air bubbles in the mixture.
6 Bake for the required time or until a skewer inserted into the centre of the cake comes out clean.
7 Allow the cake to cool in the tin. When completely cool, wrap in greaseproof paper and then in foil. Do not wrap the cake directly in foil as this can taint the taste.

Rich Fruit Cake

This is a very rich, dark cake. It is ideal for a wedding cake as it keeps very well. (c = cup/st = stick)

SHAPED TIN	15cm (6in)	18cm (7in)	20cm (8in)	23cm (9in)	25cm (10in)	28cm (11in)	30cm (12in)
SQUARE TIN	13cm (5in)	15cm (6in)	18cm (7in)	20cm (8in)	23cm (9in)	25cm (10in)	28cm (11in)
Softened butter	125g (4¼oz/1 st)	155g (5oz/1¼ st)	200g (7oz/2 st)	280g (10oz/2½ st)	410g (14½oz/3½ st)	470g (1lb 1oz/4¼ st)	625g (1lb 6oz/5½ st)
Dark muscovado sugar	125g (4¼oz/ ¾ c)	155g (5oz/ 1 c)	200g (7oz/ 1½ c)	280g (10oz/ 2 c)	410g (14½oz/ 2¾ c)	470g (1lb 1oz/ 3¼ c)	625g (1lb 6oz/ 4¼ c)
Medium eggs	2	3	3	4	6	8	9
Plain flour (all-purpose)	155g (5oz/ 1¼ c)	185g (6½oz/ 1½ c)	250g (9oz/ 2¼ c)	375g (13oz/ 3¼ c)	500g (1lb 2oz/ 4½ c)	625g (1lb 6oz/ 5½ c)	750g (1lb 10oz/ 6½ c)
Ground mixed spice (pumpkin pie spice)	1 tsp	1 tsp	1 tsp	2 tsp	3 tsp	4 tsp	6 tsp
Mixed dried fruit	440g (15½oz/ 3 c)	625g (1lb 6oz/ 4 c)	875g (1lb 15oz/ 6 c)	1.1kg (2lb 4oz/ 6¾ c)	1.5kg (3¼lb/ 9¾ c)	1.8kg (4lb/ 12 c)	2.25kg (5lb/ 15 c)
Chopped glacé cherries (candied cherries)	60g (2¼oz/ ½ c)	60g (2¼oz/ ½ c)	90g (3¼oz/ ½ c)	100g (3½oz/ ¾ c)	155g (5oz/ 1 c)	185g (6oz/ 1 c)	250g (9oz/ 1½ c)
Chopped mixed nuts	30g (1¼oz/¼ c)	30g (1¼oz/¼ c)	45g (1¾oz/½ c)	60g (2¼oz/¾ c)	90g (3¼oz/1 c)	125g (4¼oz/1 c)	185g (6½oz/1½ c)
BAKING TIME	1½–2 hrs	2–2¼ hrs	3–3¼ hrs	3½–3¾ hrs	4 hrs	4½–4¾ hrs	5–5¼ hrs

1 Preheat the oven to 140°C/275°F/Gas mark 1. Lightly grease the tin and line the base and sides with baking parchment or greaseproof paper.
2 Cream the butter and sugar together. Gradually beat in the eggs and fold in the flour and spice.
3 Stir in the mixed dried fruit, cherries and nuts until evenly combined.

4 Put the mixture into the prepared tin and level the surface. Tap the tin gently to remove any air bubbles and place in the oven.
5 Bake for the required time or until a skewer inserted into the cake comes out clean. Leave to cool in the tin, then remove and wrap firstly in greaseproof paper then tightly in foil until you are ready to decorate the cake.

Chocolate Cake

A satisfying cake for anyone who loves chocolate. (c = cup/st = stick)

SHAPED TIN	15cm (6in)	18cm (7in)	20cm (8in)	22cm (9in)	25cm (10in)	28cm (11in)	30cm (12in)	
SQUARE TIN	12cm (5in)	15cm (6in)	18cm (7in)	20cm (8in)	22cm (9in)	25cm (10in)	28cm (11in)	30cm (12in)
Softened butter	90g (3¼oz/ ¾ st)	140g (4¾oz/ 1 st)	165g (5½oz/ 1¼st)	185g (6½oz/ 1½ st)	225g (8oz/ 2 st)	325g (11½oz/ 3 st)	465g (1lb 1oz/ 4¼st)	560g (1lb 4oz/ 5 st)
Caster sugar (superfine)	165g (5½oz/ ¾ c)	250g (8¾oz/ 1¼ c)	300g (11oz/ 1½ c)	330g (11½oz/ 1½ c)	410g (14½oz/ 2 c)	570g (1lb 4oz/ 2¾ c)	660g (1lb 7oz/ 3¼ c)	825g (1lb 13oz/ 4¼ c)
Vanilla essence	1 tsp	1½ tsp	2 tsp	2½ tsp	3 tsp	4 tsp	5 tsp	6 tsp
Medium eggs	2	2	3	3	4	5	6	7
Self-raising flour	40g (1½oz/⅓ c)	55g (2oz/½ c)	65g (2½oz/9 Tbsp)	75g (3oz/⅔ c)	95g (3¼oz/¾ c)	125g (4¼oz/1 c)	150g (5oz/1¼ c)	190g (6¾oz/1½ c)
Plain flour (all-purpose)	115g (4oz/ 1 c)	165g (5½oz/ 1¼ c)	200g (7oz/ 1⅔c)	225g (8oz/ 2 c)	280g (10oz/ 2½ c)	350g (12oz/ 3 c)	445g (1lb/ 4 c)	560g (1lb 4oz/ 5 c)
Bicarbonate of soda (baking soda)	½ tsp	¾ tsp	1 tsp	1½ tsp	1¾ tsp	2¼ tsp	2½ tsp	2¾ tsp
Cocoa powder (unsweetened cocoa)	40g (1½oz/ ¼ c)	60g (2¼oz/ ½ c)	70g (2¾oz/ ½ c)	80g (3oz/ ¾ c)	90g (3¼oz/ ¾ c)	110g (3½oz/ 1 c)	120g (4¼oz/ 1 c)	160g (5½oz/ 1¼ c)
Milk	140ml (5fl oz/ ⅔ c)	210ml (7fl oz/ ¾ c)	250ml (8fl oz/ 1 c)	280ml (9fl oz/ 1 c)	350ml (11fl oz/ 1¼c)	500ml (16fl oz/ 2 c)	560ml (18fl oz/ 2¼ c)	700ml (23fl oz/ 3 c)
BAKING TIME	50 mins	1 hr	1 hr 10 mins	1¼ hrs	1 hr 20 mins	1½hrs	1 hr 40 mins	1 hr 50 mins

1 Preheat the oven to 180°C/350°F/Gas mark 4. Lightly grease the tin and line the base and sides with baking parchment or greaseproof paper.
2 Using an electric mixer, beat the butter, sugar and vanilla essence until light and fluffy.
3 Add the eggs one at a time, beating well after each addition. Transfer the mixture to a large bowl.
4 Sift the flours, bicarbonate of soda and cocoa powder into a separate bowl. Alternately add the dried mixture and the milk to the egg and butter mix.
5 Spoon the mixture into the prepared tin and level the surface. Gently tap the tin to remove any air bubbles.
6 Bake for the required time or until a skewer inserted into the cake comes out clean.
7 Leave to cool in the tin for 5 minutes before turning out onto a wire rack. Allow to cool completely.

Madeira Cake

This cake is a little firmer than a sponge and can be kept for up to a week. (c = cup/st = stick)

SHAPED TIN	15cm (6in)	18cm (7in)	20cm (8in)	23cm (9in)	25cm (10in)
SQUARE TIN	13cm (5in)	15cm (6in)	18cm (7in)	20cm (8in)	23cm (9in)
Softened butter or margarine	125g (4¼oz/1 st)	185g (6½oz/1½ st)	315g (11oz/3 st)	440g (1lb/4 st)	500g (1lb 2oz/4½ st)
Caster (superfine) sugar	125g (4¼oz/½ c)	185g (6½oz/1 c)	315g (11oz/1½ c)	440g (1lb/2¼ c)	500g (1lb 2oz/2½ c)
Medium eggs	2	3	5	7	8
Self-raising flour	185g (6½oz/1½ c)	250g (8¾oz/2 c)	375g (13oz/3¼ c)	500g (1lb 2oz/4¼ c)	625g (1lb 6oz/5½ c)
BAKING TIME	1–1¾ hrs	1¼–1½ hrs	1½–1¾ hrs	1¾–2 hrs	2 hrs
Flavourings					
Ground mixed spice (pumpkin pie spice)	1 tsp	1 tsp	1½ tsp	2 tsp	3 tsp
Grated zest of lemon, orange or lime	1 fruit	2 fruits	3 fruits	4 fruits	5 fruits
Chopped mixed nuts	30g (1¼oz/¾ c)	60g (2¼oz/1 c)	90g (3¼oz/1 c)	125g (4¼oz/1¼ c)	155g (5oz/1½ c)

1 Preheat the oven to 160°C/325°F/Gas mark 3. Lightly grease the tin and line it with baking parchment or greaseproof paper.
2 Put the butter or margarine, sugar, eggs and flour into a mixing bowl and mix with a wooden spoon. Beat for 2–3 minutes until the mixture is smooth and glossy.
3 Put the mixture into the tin and smooth the top with a spatula. Tap the tin to remove any air bubbles.
4 Bake in the centre of the oven for the required time or until a skewer inserted into the centre comes out clean. When the cake is cooked it should be golden brown on the top and will have a slight crust.
5 Leave the cake to cool completely on a wire rack.

Carrot cake

This is a classic favourite. I have put this recipe in because more and more people are having carrot cake as one of the tiers of their wedding cake. It's a nice alternative to fruit cake or madeira sponge. However, it is not a very dense cake so I would advise using it only as a top tier in a stacked or pillared cake.

(Makes a 20cm/8in square cake)
125g (4½oz/1 cup) self-raising flour
Pinch of salt
1 tsp ground cinnamon
125g (4½oz/¾ cup) soft brown sugar
2 medium eggs, beaten
100ml (3½fl oz/scant ½ cup) sunflower oil
125g (4½oz/¾ cup) carrots, peeled and finely grated
1 banana, roughly mashed
25g (1oz/¼ cup) walnuts, chopped

1 Preheat the oven to 180°C/350°F/Gas mark 4. Lightly grease a 20cm (8in) square cake tin and line it with greaseproof paper.
2 Sieve the flour, salt and ground cinnamon into a large bowl. Stir in the brown sugar. Add the beaten eggs and oil. Mix the ingredients together well.
3 Stir in the grated carrot, mashed banana and chopped walnuts until well combined.
4 Pour the mixture into the tin and bake for 20–25 minutes or until just firm to the touch. Leave in the tin to cool on a wire rack.

The top tier of Coronet and Cushions is a carrot cake (see pages 62–65).

Filling and Icing Recipes

All of these fillings and icings are available to buy ready-made if you do not wish to make your own.

Buttercream

Buttercream is a versatile filling, icing and frosting, which can be spread easily or piped.

(Makes 1 quantity)
250g (9oz/scant 2 cups) icing (confectioner's) sugar
115g (4oz/1 stick) softened butter
10ml (2 tsp) boiled water

1 Sift the icing sugar thoroughly.
2 Place the butter in a bowl and beat until pale and fluffy.
3 Add the icing sugar a little at a time, beating well after each addition.
4 Beat in the water and any flavouring you may require (see below).

Alternatively, place all of the ingredients into a food processor and blend for 30 seconds.

Flavourings

Flavourings can be added if desired; here are a few suggestions:
Vanilla – add 5ml (1 tsp) vanilla essence.
Citrus – beat in 2 tsp finely grated lemon, orange or lime zest.
Coffee – dissolve 4 tsp instant coffee in 2 tsp of boiled water.
Almond – beat in 1 tsp almond essence and 2 Tbsp chopped, toasted almonds.
Chocolate – beat in 30g (1oz) sifted cocoa powder (unsweetened cocoa) or 50g (2oz) melted dark (semisweet) chocolate.
Liqueur – add 3 tsp of your chosen liqueur.

Chocolate Buttercream

Work quickly with this recipe as it sets quite firmly. You may find it easier if you keep the mixture slightly warm by standing it over a bowl of hot water.

(Makes 1 quantity)
200g (8oz) dark (semisweet) chocolate (50% cocoa solids)
100g (4oz/1 stick) unsalted (sweet) butter (at room temp.)
200g (8oz/1½ cups) icing (confectioner's) sugar

1 Break the chocolate into small pieces and melt in the microwave or place in a heatproof bowl over a pan of hot water and heat gently.
2 Put the butter in a mixing bowl. Add the icing sugar, sifting it as you add. Add the melted chocolate.
3 Beat everything together until very light and fluffy.

Sugarpaste (Rolled Fondant)

I recommend that you use ready-made sugarpaste, however, here is a recipe if you prefer to make your own. Always roll out sugarpaste on a work surface lightly dusted with icing (confectioner's) sugar.

(Makes 1 quantity)
1 egg white (see note page 4) or make up using dried egg white
30ml (2 tsp) liquid glucose
625g (1lb 6oz/3¾ cups) icing (confectioner's) sugar
A little white vegetable fat or shortening

1 Put the egg white and liquid glucose into a bowl.
2 Sift the icing sugar into the bowl, adding a little at a time. Stir continuously and the mixture will thicken.
3 Put the mixture onto a work surface lightly dusted with icing sugar. Knead until smooth and soft. If you find it is a little dry, knead in a little white vegetable fat or shortening. The paste should be soft and pliable.
4 Wrap in clingfilm and put in a food-safe plastic bag to rest. Store in an airtight container if not using straightaway.

Colouring Sugarpaste (Rolled Fondant)

1 Knead the sugarpaste thoroughly.
2 Add a little of the food colouring to the sugarpaste using a cocktail stick (pic a).
3 Knead the sugarpaste well until all the colour has been absorbed (pic b).
4 Add a little more food colouring if a deeper colour is required.
5 Wrap the sugarpaste until required.

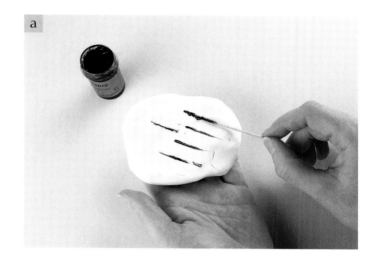

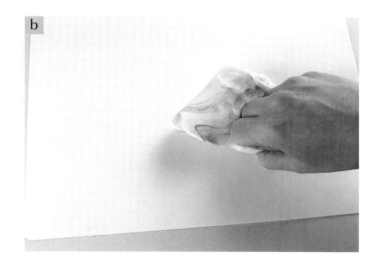

Royal Icing

Royal icing can be used to cover a cake but it is quite time consuming, therefore I haven't used it to cover any of the cakes in this book. I have used it for piping fine decoration and attaching decoration to a cake covered in sugarpaste. An alternative recipe is provided below which uses dried egg white (see note page 4). Keep the icing in the fridge, but the mixture will need to be re-beaten before use.

(Makes 1 quantity)
2 egg whites (see note page 4)
1ml (¼ tsp) lemon juice
450g (1lb/3¼ cups) icing (confectioner's) sugar
5ml (1 tsp) glycerine (optional)

1 Place the egg whites and lemon juice into a bowl. Stir with a wooden spoon to break up the egg whites.
2 Sieve the icing sugar thoroughly and add approximately one third to the egg whites and mix well.
3 Continue mixing, adding the sugar a little at a time until you reach the consistency you require. The mixture should be smooth, glossy and light in texture.
4 Add glycerine to the mixture if you are using the icing for coating or if a softer icing is required. The icing should be light and fluffy.
5 Place the icing into a sealable container and directly cover the surface of the icing with clingfilm before placing on the lid. Keep for a maximum of two days.

Alternative Royal Icing Recipe

10g (½oz) dried egg white
60ml (4 Tbsp) water
450g (1lb/3 cups) icing (confectioner's) sugar
5ml (1 tsp) glycerine

1 Mix the dried egg white and water together thoroughly in a small container. Leave to stand for about 5 minutes.
2 Sieve the icing sugar thoroughly.
3 Sieve the dried-egg white mixture into a large mixing bowl and add one third of the icing sugar. Mix until the icing sugar is absorbed.
4 Continue adding small amounts of sugar until it has all been used, mixing well after each addition.
5 If you are using the icing for coating add the glycerine to the mixture and mix well.
6 Place the icing into a sealable container and directly cover the surface of the icing with clingfilm before placing on the lid.

Making a Piping (Decorating) Bag

1 Cut some greaseproof paper into a triangle.

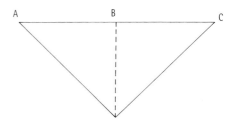

2 Pick up corner C and fold over, so that B forms a sharp cone in the centre.

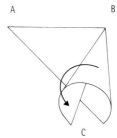

3 Wrap corner A around the cone. Make sure that A and C are at the back and that the point of the cone is sharp.

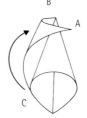

4 Fold points A and C inside the top edge of the bag to hold it securely. Snip off the end B and insert a piping tube (nozzle).

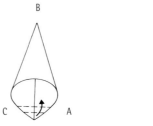 

Colouring Royal Icing

You can use various products to colour your icing but do make sure the correct consistency is maintained.

1 Mix the icing thoroughly.
2 Add the food colouring to the royal icing a little at a time using a cocktail stick (pic a).
3 Stir or mix the colouring into the icing until blended (pic b).
4 Leave the icing to stand to allow the colour to mature.
5 Place icing into a sealable container. Directly cover the surface of the icing with clingfilm before placing on the lid.

Marzipan

Marzipan forms a smooth coating on a cake and makes a perfect base for sugarpaste or royal icing, forming a barrier that prevents moisture seeping from the cake into the coating. For modelling the paste is easy to handle and can be coloured in the same way as sugarpaste (see page 15). Store in a food-safe plastic bag until ready for use. It is advisable to use the marzipan within one week.

225g (8oz/1½ cups) icing (confectioner's) sugar
225g (8oz/1½ cups) ground almonds
1 large egg white (see note page 4)
1 tsp lemon juice
Few drops almond essence (extract)

1 Place the icing sugar and almonds into a bowl, add the egg white, lemon juice and almond essence and stir together.
2 Knead the mixture until smooth on a surface dusted with icing sugar.

Flower Paste

Flower paste dries hard and is used for making flowers and leaves. For this recipe you will need an electric mixer.

450g (1lb/3¼ cups) icing (confectioner's) sugar
15ml (3 tsp) gum tragacanth
10ml (2 tsp) powdered gelatine
25ml (5 tsp) cold water
10ml (2 tsp) white vegetable fat (shortening)
10ml (2 tsp) liquid glucose
1 large egg white (see note page 4)

1 Sift the icing sugar and gum tragacanth.
2 Place the icing sugar and gum tragacanth together into a mixing bowl and warm in a very low oven (150°C/300°F/Gas mark 2) for around 5 minutes.
3 Dissolve the gelatine in the cold water and leave to stand until no grains are left.
4 Add the vegetable fat and liquid glucose to the gelatine.
5 Dissolve over hot (not boiling) water or in a microwave on defrost or the lowest setting (do not allow to boil).
6 Put the icing sugar into a warmed bowl and add the gelatine mixture and egg white.
7 Mix together until white and "stringy".
8 Knead the mixture together by hand, then knead on a work surface lightly dusted with icing sugar.
9 Wrap in two layers of clingfilm and place in a food-safe plastic bag. Leave to stand for 24 hours before using.

Flower Paste Glue

This is a clear glue and is mainly used to secure wire in flowers and leaves.

1.25ml (¼ tsp) Tylo powder (a thickener)
Water

1 Put the Tylo powder into a small, sealable jar. Cover the powder with cold water and leave to dissolve.
2 Stir until the mixture is thick and clear. Add more water or powder to achieve the correct consistency.
3 Place the top on the jar. The mixture is ready for use as required.

Modelling Paste

This is a paste for making models and decorations. Gum tragacanth acts as a strengthening agent, so it sets much harder than sugarpaste and holds its shape. If rolling out the paste work on a surface dusted with a little icing sugar. When modelling small pieces use a smear of white vegetable fat on your fingers to prevent sticking.

280g (10oz/2 cups) icing (confectioner's) sugar
3 tsp gum tragacanth
1 tsp liquid glucose
6 tsp cold water
315g (11oz) sugarpaste (rolled fondant)

1 Sieve together the icing sugar and gum tragacanth.
2 Add the liquid glucose and 6 teaspoons of cold water and mix thoroughly.
3 Knead the mixture to form soft dough, then combine this with an equal weight of sugarpaste. The paste should feel just like sugarpaste.
4 If the mixture is too dry, use a little white vegetable fat to make it soft and pliable. If the mixture is too sticky, then knead in a little sifted icing sugar.

Ganache

Ganache can be used whipped as a filling or coating, or warmed for a pour-over coating.

225g (8oz) dark (semisweet) chocolate, broken into small pieces
150ml (4½fl oz/½ cup) whipping cream

1 Put the chocolate pieces in a heatproof bowl.
2 Put the cream in a pan and heat gently until boiling.
3 Remove from the heat and pour over the chocolate.
4 Stir until the chocolate is melted and has blended into a dark mixture. Pour into a clean bowl and allow to set.
5 To pour over a cake, gently warm the ganache.
6 For piping, or filling a cake, whip until light and fluffy.

Modelling chocolate

Modelling chocolate is used when you want something made out of chocolate to hold its shape and form.

500g (17oz) baking chocolate, broken into pieces
110ml (4fl oz/½ cup) liquid glucose
50ml (2fl oz/¼ cup) sugar water

1 Melt the chocolate in a heatproof bowl over a saucepan of hot water.
2 Put the liquid glucose and sugar water into a heatproof bowl over a saucepan of hot water.
3 Add the warm glucose mixture to the melted chocolate and gently stir with a spoon. Do not beat.
4 Pour the mixture into a food-safe plastic bag and leave to stand at room temperature for 24 hours before using.

Tip

To make sugar water, add 4 parts granulated sugar to 3 parts water. Put it in a saucepan and bring to the boil to dissolve the sugar. Leave to cool.

Cake Preparation

Before you decorate your cake you need to prepare it in the correct way.

Sugarpaste (Rolled Fondant)

If you are covering a madeira cake with sugarpaste you need to coat it with a layer of buttercream or jam (jelly). If you are using a fruit cake it should first be covered with a layer of marzipan.

How to Marzipan a Cake for Sugarpaste

The marzipan-covered cake needs to be left to dry for about seven days before covering with sugarpaste.

1 Place the cake on a board.

2 Spread the top and sides with warm apricot glaze.

3 Sprinkle your work surface with sieved icing sugar.

4 Knead the marzipan into a smooth ball (do not over-knead as this will bring the oils to the surface) and roll out in the shape of the cake to 5mm (¼in) thick, allowing enough for the top and sides of the cake. Make sure the marzipan moves freely, then lift gently and place evenly onto the cake.

5 Smooth the marzipan over the top and down the sides of the cake using your hands.

6 Use a cake smoother to mould the marzipan firmly to the top and sides of the cake (pic a).

7 Use a sharp knife to trim off the excess marzipan from the base of the cake, cutting down onto the board (pic b).

Tips

To make apricot glaze – sieve apricot jam to remove any large lumps of fruit. Heat gently until it is of a runny consistency.

Marzipan creates the smooth foundation for the sugarpaste. Therefore it is important to take the time to apply it neatly.

Covering a Cake with Sugarpaste

Once you have prepared the cake in the correct way (see page 19), you are now ready to cover the cake with sugarpaste.

1 If you are covering a marzipan-covered fruit cake, dampen the marzipan with clear alcohol or boiled water.

2 Sprinkle the work surface with icing sugar. Knead the sugarpaste into a smooth ball.

3 Roll out the sugarpaste, allowing for the top and sides of the cake, and add a little extra width if you are covering the board at the same time.

4 Gently lift the sugarpaste and place it centrally on the cake.

5 Use your hands to gently press the sugarpaste onto the cake. Start at the top and carefully smooth down the sides.

6 Use a cake smoother to firmly mould the paste (pic a).

7 Trim off any excess paste at the base of the cake. If covering the cake and board in one go, smooth the icing on the board and trim off the excess around the board (pic b).

Covering a Cake Board with Sugarpaste

The cake board can be covered at the same time as the cake (see page 19), or follow the method below.

1 Roll out the sugarpaste to the shape of board.

2 Slightly dampen the board with clear alcohol or cooled, boiled water and carefully lift the sugarpaste over the board. Smooth with a cake smoother and emboss if desired.

3 Cut off any excess paste and leave to dry (pic c).

The board for the Chocolate Heart is covered with sugarpaste at the same time as the cake (see page 31).

Assembling the Cake

Many of the cake designs in this book are tiered or stacked, or include stands and separators. It is very important that you assemble the cake correctly so that it is secure and stable.

Assembling a Cake with Pillars

It's very important that you are work on a level surface.

1 Make a greaseproof paper template of the top of each cake that is going to have pillars on it. For example — if the design has three tiers, make templates of the bottom and middle tier cakes.

2 Work out the position of the pillars by folding the template and then unfolding it to leave guidelines. Mark the position of the pillars on the template on the guidelines. The information shown right and on pages 22–23 shows you how many pillars you need and where they should be positioned for a variety of cake shapes.

3 Place the template on top of the cake. Mark where the pillars will go by pressing a scriber onto the top of the cake.

4 Place all of the pillars in position. Rest a spirit (carpenter's) level on top of the pillars to see if they are level. If you find that they are slightly uneven, for step 5 use the highest one as the guide. Take the pillars off the cake.

5 Insert a dowel straight down into the cake until it reaches the cake board. Drop a pillar over the dowel then mark where the top of the pillar comes on the dowel with a pencil. Remove the pillar and dowel.

6 Cut the dowel where you made the mark using a small hacksaw or I use a small plumber's pipe cutter. Cut as many dowels as you need to the same length. Place each dowel in position in the cake with the end that has been cut at the top and not in the cake. Place the pillars over the top of the dowels.

7 Repeat this procedure for each tier, then assemble the tiers centrally on top of each other, lining up the pillars.

Square Cake

Four pillars placed in a cross shape (A) or at the corners (B).

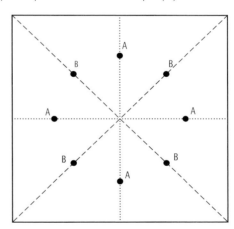

Round Cake

Use either three or four pillars.

Three pillars (A) — use a protractor to measure three points at 120-degree angles for guidelines.

Four pillars (B) — fold the template in half, then half again.

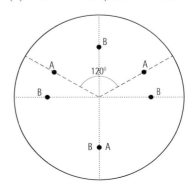

Petal-shaped Cake

Use three pillars. Use a protractor to measure three points at 120-degree angles, either from the middle of the inner (A) or the outer (B) curve of the petal.

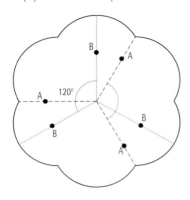

Hexagonal Cake

Three pillars positioned in a triangle. Use a protractor to measure three points at 120-degree angles for guidelines; from the middle of the flat edge (A) or from the points (B).

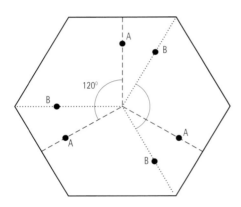

Triangular Cake

Three pillars – fold (B) to (C), this gives you the centre line. Unfold. Fold (A) to (B), unfold. Fold (A) to (C), unfold.

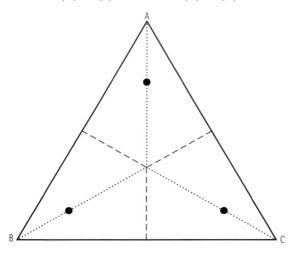

Oval Cake

Use either three or four pillars.
Three pillars – use a protractor to mark three points at 120-degree angles for guidelines.
Four pillars – fold in half and half again in either a cross shape (A) or on the diagonal (B).

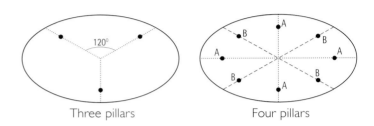

Three pillars   Four pillars

Heart-shaped Cake

Three pillars – fold the heart in half lengthways (A), then fold the point up level with the top of the cake (B). Unfold (C). Put a protractor on the central vertical fold at the point of the heart and mark a 120-degree angle on one side of the line. Turn the protractor around and measure a 120-degree angle on the other side of the line.

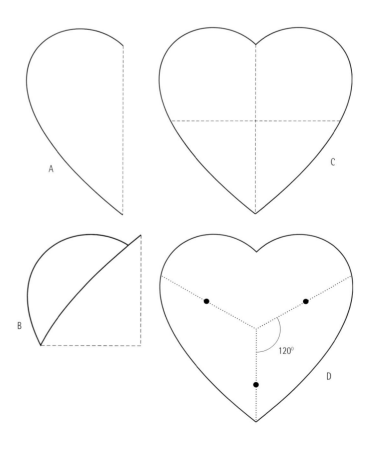

When marking the position of the pillars on the guidelines measure from the centre point out. Use this as a guide as to where to put the pillars on the guidelines

Size of the cake	distance of pillar from centre
20cm (8in)	64mm (2½in)
25cm (10in)	76mm (3in)
30cm (12in)	89mm (3½in)
36cm (14in)	102mm (4in)

Stacked Cakes

I would recommend that you support all stacked cakes with dowels, especially madeira and chocolate cakes. Only the supporting tiers need to have dowels inserted into them, the top tier doesn't need them.

1 To make things easier, I'm going to use the example of a three-tier cake. You will need two greaseproof paper templates – one of the middle tier and one of the top tier.
2 Divide the templates equally into six. Make a mark on each division 13mm (½in) in from the edge. This is where the dowel will be inserted. Place the template of the middle tier centrally onto the bottom tier cake and mark the points where the dowels will be inserted by pressing onto the top of the cake with a scriber.
3 Insert one dowel into the cake, right down to the cake board. Make a mark on the dowel, level with the top of the cake. Remove the dowel and cut where you made the mark. Cut six dowels to the same size. Now place into the cake.
4 Repeat steps 2 and 3 for the middle tier cake, using the top tier template. Stack each cake centrally on top of the one below. Then, with the same colour royal icing or sugarpaste mixed with cooled, boiled water to achieve a piping consistency, fill the gaps between the joins.

So, basically you need to use a template of the tier above for the cake below.

Using Separators

Separators come in many shapes and sizes. When using separators between the tiers it is advisable to insert dowels into the cake just underneath the separators for extra support.

1 Position the separator centrally on the sugarpaste-covered cake. Press down gently to leave a slight mark in the paste. Remove the separator.
2 Insert a dowel into the cake, just inside the marked area. Make a mark on the dowel level with the top of the cake. Remove the dowel and cut where you made the mark. Cut at least three more dowels to the same size.
3 Insert the dowels into the cake, right through to the board, making sure they are evenly spaced. Place the separator in position and stack the cakes.

Stands

There are a wide choice of stands available with a varying number of tiers, and they can be straight, spiral, offset, and made of metal or acrylic. Using a stand is a simple but effective way of displaying your cake and it means that you don't have to worry about using dowels or pillars.

Swags and Roses is displayed on a two-tier "C" stand (see pages 102–105).

Cake Designs

There are 22 cake designs for you to choose from, ranging from single-tier to four-tier, classic white to funky pink. There's a design to suit every wedding.

Enchanting
Butterflies

I made this cake in traditional white because I feel it is so elegant,

but if you prefer you could colour the butterflies.

Materials

20cm (8in) and 30cm (12in) oval light fruit cakes
(see page 11)

Apricot glaze

2.25kg (5lb) marzipan (see page 17)

Clear alcohol or boiled water

2.625kg (5lb 12oz) white sugarpaste (rolled fondant)

150g (5oz) flower paste (see page 17)

Petal base (Jem)

Edible glue

Royal icing (see page 16)

Equipment

23cm (9in) and 38cm (15in) oval cake drum boards

Rolling pin

Sharp knife

Cake smoother

Closed scallop serrated crimpers

Butterfly cutter set

Non-stick board

3 A4 (8 x 12in) sheets of thin card

76mm (3in) high tubular separator

Paintbrush

Piping (decorating) bag fitted with no. 1.5 piping
tube (nozzle)

26g silver wire

Two fine posy picks

Double-sided tape

White ribbon for cake drum board

4 dowels

1 Place the 20cm (8in) cake on the 23cm (9in) drum board and the 30cm (12in) cake on the 38cm (15in) drum board. Cover the cakes with marzipan (see page 19). Cover the cakes and boards with sugarpaste (see page 20).

2 While the paste is still soft, crimp the outer edges of the boards. Then, using a medium-sized butterfly cutter, emboss all the way around the top outer edge of the bottom tier cake (you should fit in 18 butterflies, pic a). Emboss around the side of the top tier with the large butterfly cutter (you should fit in eight butterflies). Leave to dry.

3 Roll out the flower paste on a non-stick board lightly greased with petal base. Grease the medium and large butterfly cutters with petal base and cut out 24 large and 12 medium butterflies (pic b). Concertina the sheets of thin card and open out. Place all but four of the large butterflies into the folds (refer to pic d); this will lift the wings. Leave to dry.

4 Use the four large butterflies that you set aside in step 3 to decorate the separator. Secure in place with edible glue or water (pic c).

5 Place the medium-sized butterflies around the top of the top tier, securing in place with royal icing (pic d). Place 18 large butterflies around the side of the bottom tier and fix in position with royal icing.

6 Cut two lengths of silver wire – one 15cm (6in) long and the other 9cm (3½in). Add a small sausage of flower paste to the back of the bodies of the two remaining large butterflies. Dampen the paste with a little edible glue, then place a wire into the paste on each butterfly. Leave to dry.

7 Place the posy picks into the centre of the top tier, about 5cm (2in) apart. Fill the posy picks with royal icing and insert a wired butterfly into each. Bend each wire so the butterflies look as if they are flying.

8 Stick double-sided tape around the cake drum board and trim with ribbon. Assemble the cakes, referring to page 23 for using the separator.

Chocolate *Heart*

Using white and dark chocolate makes this a delightfully effective cake. This understated, single tier cake would be ideal for an informal wedding. It could also be used for birthdays and anniversaries.

Materials

25cm (10in) heart-shaped chocolate cake (see pages 12–13)

1 quantity chocolate buttercream or ganache (see pages 15 and 18)

Jam (jelly) (optional)

1.5kg (3lb 4oz) chocolate-flavoured sugarpaste (rolled fondant)

Cooled, boiled water

150g (5oz) white modelling chocolate (see page 18) or white cocoform

Equipment

Sharp knife

Palette knife

33cm (13in) heart cake drum board

Rolling pin

Cake smoother

Petal veining tool

Non-stick board or marble slab

Arum lily cutters

Heatproof bowl

Saucepan

Double-sided tape

Brown ribbon for cake drum board

1 Cut the cake in half horizontally and fill with chocolate buttercream and jam if desired. Fix in the centre of the drum board using a little chocolate buttercream. Coat the cake evenly with a thin layer of buttercream using a palette knife.

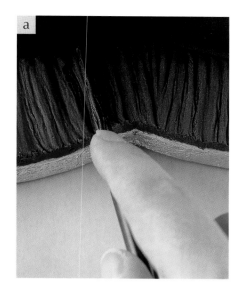

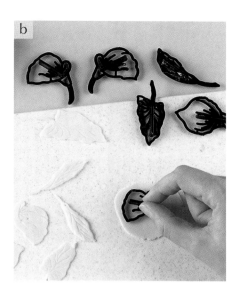

2 Roll the sugarpaste out into a circle large enough to cover the cake and drum board. Dampen the edges of the board with a little boiled water.

3 Place the sugarpaste centrally onto the top of the cake, easing it down the side of the cake and onto the board. Smooth the cake and the board using a cake smoother. (See page 20.)

4 To texture the board, rock the veining tool backwards and forwards over the sugarpaste, all the way around the base of the cake (pic a).

Tip

To melt the modelling chocolate, put a small amount into a heatproof bowl over a pan of water (the bowl should not touch the water). Heat gently until the modelling chocolate melts.

5 Roll out the white modelling chocolate to about 2mm (⅛in) thick on a non-stick board. Cut out a variety of arum lilies and leaves (pic b).

6 Arrange the lilies and leaves on the top and sides of the cake (pic c) so that most of the surface is covered. Secure with a little melted white modelling chocolate (see Tip left).

7 Stick double-sided tape around the cake drum board and trim with ribbon.

Double *Heart*

With romance in the air what could be more fitting than a double heart wedding cake? This design would be perfect for the couple who are looking for an unusual single-tier cake. I have used readymade sugarcraft flowers, but of course, you could make your own.

Materials

Two 23cm (9in) heart-shaped madeira cakes
(see page 13)

3 quantities of buttercream (see page 14)

Jam (jelly) (optional)

1.5kg (3lb 4oz) violet sugarpaste (rolled fondant)

2 small sugarcraft lily bouquets

1 large sugarcraft lily bouquet

Equipment

Sharp knife

Palette knife

46cm (18in) double heart cake drum board

Rolling pin

Bubble texture roller

Ribbon cutter

Piping (decorating) bag fitted with no. 2 piping tube
(nozzle)

244cm (8ft) violet twisted rope with silver beads

Dove on double gold ring decoration

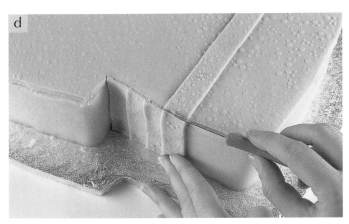

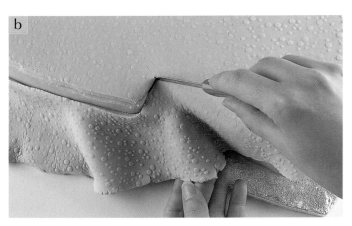

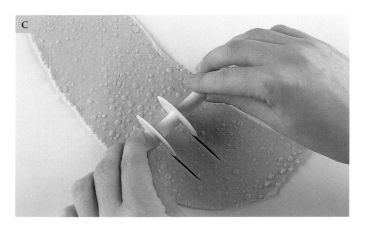

1 Cut one of the cakes to shape following the cutting guide on page 110. Cut the cakes in half and fill with buttercream and jam if desired. Place the cakes onto the drum board, fitting them together. Cover with a thin layer of buttercream.

2 Roll out a piece of sugarpaste 43 x 30cm (17 x 12in). Texture with the bubble texture roller (pic a). Place the sugarpaste on top of the cake, then trim around the top of the cake, removing the excess (pic b).

3 Roll out some more sugarpaste and texture as before. Using the ribbon cutter set on 25mm (1in) wide, cut out long strips (pic c). Starting at the joining point of the two hearts (pic d), place the end of a strip on the board and then smooth the paste up the side of the cake. Cut the strip level with the top of the cake. Continue around the cake, overlapping the strips as you go.

4 Take a small amount of sugarpaste, add a little cooled, boiled water to it and mix until it is of a piping consistency. Put in the piping bag and pipe around the bottom of the cake. Starting at the back of the cake, place the twisted rope in position (pic e). I always bind the ends of the rope so they will not come undone. Do the same on the top of the cake, making sure it is neat.

5 Place the large bouquet and one small bouquet together on the top of the cake. Position the second small bouquet on the board, to one side. Put the double ring decoration on the top of the cake, towards the bottom right and secure with the piping consistency sugarpaste. (Refer to photo on page 33.)

She Sells *Seashells*

For this cake I have used ready-made Belgian chocolate seashells. If you would like to make your own chocolates there are lots of different moulds on the market.

Materials

15cm (6in), 20cm (8in) and 25cm (10in) round chocolate cakes (see page 12–13)

Jam (jelly) (optional)

4 quantities of chocolate buttercream or ganache (see pages 14 and 18)

3kg (6lb 8oz) chocolate-flavoured sugarpaste (rolled fondant)

100g (3½oz) white modelling chocolate (see page 18) or white cocoform

60g (2¼oz) white chocolate curls

Three white cigarellos

Selection of chocolate seashells

Equipment

36cm (14in) round cake drum board

15cm (6in) and 20cm (8in) thin cake boards

Sharp knife

Palette knife

Rolling pin

Cake smoother

12 dowels

Non-stick board or marble slab

Leaf cutters

Heatproof bowl

Saucepan

Double-sided tape

Brown ribbon for cake drum board

1. Put the largest cake on the drum board and the other two tiers on the appropriate thin boards. Cut the cakes in half horizontally and fill with jam if liked. Coat the cakes with chocolate buttercream or ganache. Cover the largest cake and board in one with sugarpaste. Cover the other cakes with sugarpaste. (See page 20.)

2. The cakes need to be supported with dowels. Follow the instructions on page 23. Carefully stack the cakes.

3. Roll out the white modelling chocolate on a non-stick board. Cut out a selection of leaves (pic a) – the leaves represent seaweed! Place randomly up the sides of the cake (refer to main photo left), securing with melted white chocolate. (Melt some of the white chocolate curls. See page 31 for how to melt chocolate.)

4. Cut three large pieces of seaweed (leaves) for the top tier decoration. Stick a cigarello to the back of each piece of seaweed with some melted white chocolate (pic b). Set aside.

5. Sprinkle some white chocolate curls at the base of the cake, then start arranging the chocolate seashells up the cake, securing with melted chocolate (melt some of the seashells) (pic c).

6. Push the three seaweed pieces set aside in step 4 into the top of the cake. Stick a couple of chocolate seashells onto the seaweed.

7. Stick double-sided tape around the edge of the drum board and trim with ribbon.

Tip

It is important to keep this cake cool and when displaying the cake be aware of sunlight coming through windows and any other sources of heat.

Baskets
of Flowers

Using this tiered floral centrepiece is a good way of introducing fresh or artificial flowers to a cake. If you are going to use fresh flowers, as I have, you must read the tips on page 41 before you start.

Materials

20 x 11.5cm (8 x 4½in) deep and 13 x 9cm (5 x 3½in) deep round rich fruit cakes (see page 12)

Apricot glaze

1.5kg (3lb 4oz) marzipan (see page 17)

500g (1lb 2oz) white sugarpaste (rolled fondant) for the drum board

Clear alcohol or boiled water

1.5kg (3lb 4oz) white sugarpaste (rolled fondant) for the cakes

Equipment

30cm (12in) round cake drum board

13cm (5in) thin cake board

Rolling pin

Sharp knife

Cake smoother

Closed vee serrated crimpers

Basketweave textured roller

12 dowels

Pencil

13cm (5in) and 20cm (8in) diameter flower holders

Selection of fresh flowers (see Tips on page 41)

Double-sided tape

White ribbon for cake drum board

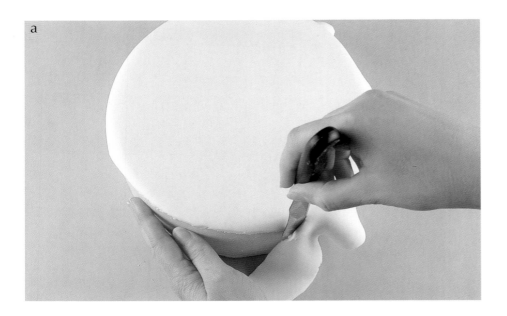

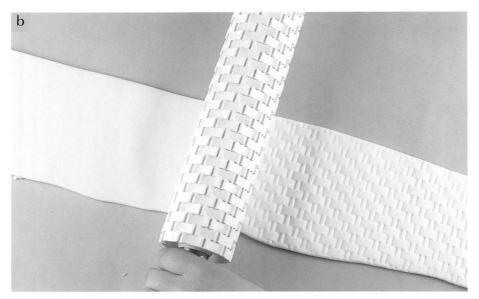

1 Place the large cake centrally onto the drum board and the small cake on the thin cake board. Cover each cake with marzipan (see page 19).

2 Roll out the white sugarpaste for the drum board into a strip, approximately 97 × 8cm (38 × 3in). Dampen the base of the board with a little water then place the strip on the board, curving it around the cake. Overlap the ends slightly and trim. Work the two ends together so that you cannot see the join. Smooth the sugarpaste with a cake smoother. Trim any excess paste from around the edge of the drum board. Crimp the edge.

3 Roll out enough sugarpaste to cover the tops of both cakes. Dampen the top of the cakes with either clear alcohol or boiled water and then place the sugarpaste on top. Trim any excess paste with a sharp knife (pic a).

4 Measure the depth of the large cake. Roll out a strip of sugarpaste approximately 65cm (26in) long by the depth of the cake. Texture with the basketweave texture roller (pic b). Trim the edges straight.

5 Dampen the sides of the cake with either clear alcohol or boiled water and place the paste around the cake (pic c). Trim the ends and join them together (make this the back of the cake). Repeat this procedure for the small cake; the paste needs to be approximately 43cm (17in) long.

6 As this is a stacked design, the cakes need to be supported with dowels (pic d). See page 23 for instructions. In the case of this cake your templates need to be the same size as the flower holder that sits on top of the cake.

7 Fill the flower holders with water and arrange the flowers (pic e).

8 Carefully place the large flower holder on top of the large cake, then sit the small cake in the middle of the large holder. Place the small flower holder on top.

9 Stick double-sided tape around the edge of the drum board and trim with ribbon.

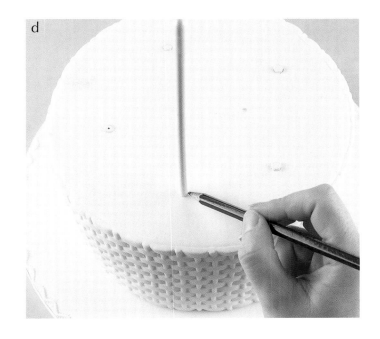

Tips

- *The flowers should be arranged and the cake assembled on the wedding day at the reception venue.*
- *Don't move the cake after flower holders have been filled with water.*
- *Dismantle the cake carefully before cutting.*

When using fresh flowers on a cake:

- *Check with your florist that the type of flowers you want to use are suitable for use on a cake as many flowers and their leaves are poisonous.*
- *Many purchased flowers are sprayed with pesticides. Ask for pesticide-free flowers.*
- *Never put fresh flowers directly on a cake; use separator plates, floral holders, greaseproof paper or doilies to keep the flowers from touching the cake.*
- *Never insert stems directly into the cake.*

Pretty
Blossom

I would advise you to make the blossom flowers in advance for this pretty cake. Although simple to make, they will take you a little time.

Materials

1 heaped tsp gum tragacanth (or suitable substitute)

2.25kg (5lb) white sugarpaste (rolled fondant)

Paste colours: primrose, pink, violet, mint green, baby blue

Petal base or white vegetable fat

Edible glitter flakes: snow, pink, violet, green, blue,

Royal icing (see page 16)

Harlequin dragees

3 madeira cakes (baked in pudding basins) 15cm (6in), 20cm (8in) and 25cm (10in) (see page 13)

3 quantities of buttercream (see page 14)

Jam (jelly) (optional)

Equipment

Rolling pin

26mm (1in) blossom cutter

Balling tool

Sheets of dimpled foam

Piping (decorating) bag fitted with no. 1.5 piping tube (nozzle)

Cranked tweezers

15cm (6in), 20cm (8in) and 25cm (10in) thin, round cake boards

Sharp knife and palette knife

Cake smoother

Green ribbon, 4cm (1½in) wide

Double-sided tape

3 tier acrylic stand

1 Add the gum tragacanth to 400g (14oz) white sugarpaste. Divide the sugarpaste into five equal pieces and colour each piece with one of the paste colours (see page 15). Roll each piece of coloured sugarpaste out and cut out the blossoms (pic a). You will need approximately 500 blossoms to decorate the three cakes. This quantity allows for some breakages.

2 While the blossoms are still damp, ball each petal in towards the centre; this will give the blossoms a cupped shape. Place the blossoms on the dimpled foam sheets and leave to dry (pic b).

3 When dry, smear each blossom with petal base. Sprinkle the blossoms with the appropriate coloured edible glitter flakes (pic c).

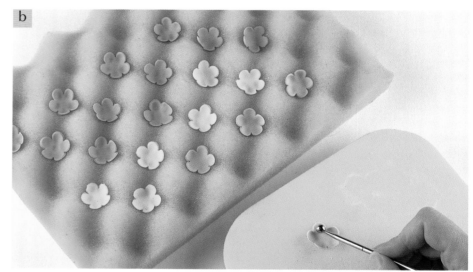

Tip

The dimpled foam sheets that you use should be new and not previously used for any other purpose.

4 Place the royal icing in the piping bag. Pipe a small dot in the centre of each blossom and add one of the harlequin dragees using the cranked tweezers (pic d).

5 Place each cake on the corresponding board. If liked, cut each cake in half horizontally and fill with buttercream and jam. Coat the cakes with buttercream. Roll out the remaining white sugarpaste and cover each cake (see page 20).

6 Place the blossoms all over the cakes, securing in place with royal icing (pic e). The blossoms should be quite tightly packed together.

7 To make the "leaves" for the uprights of the stand, cut four strips of green ribbon and cut one end of each strip so that it resembles a leaf shape. Stick double-sided tape three-quarters of the way up each strip and stick to the uprights of the stand. Put the cakes in place on the stand.

8 Cut a couple of short pieces of green ribbon, shape the ends as before and tuck these under the large cake.

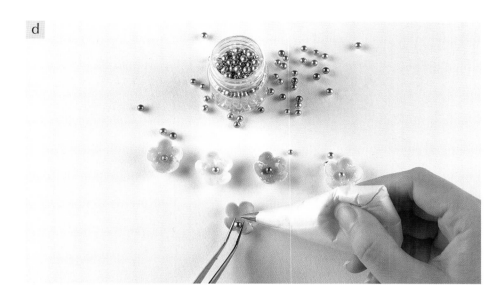

Tip

There are many different stands on the market, so have a look around and choose the one you prefer. Stands can be expensive to buy, so try hiring one from a cake decorating shop instead.

Burgundy
Rose Drape

This two-tier cake is ideal for the smaller wedding, but the design could easily be adapted and more tiers added. With its fabric-effect drape and dramatic burgundy roses, it is simple but stylish.

Materials

25cm (10in) oval and 10cm (4in) round light fruit cake (see page 11)

Apricot glaze

1.5kg (3lb 4oz) marzipan (see page 17)

Clear alcohol or boiled water

2.25kg (5lb) ivory sugarpaste (rolled fondant)

Ivory-coloured royal icing (see page 16)

Equipment

36 x 30cm (14 x 12in) oval cake drum board

Rolling pin

Sharp knife

Cake smoother

Closed triple scallop crimpers

10cm (4in) round thin cake board

Piping (decorating) bag fitted with no. 2 piping tube (nozzle)

Ribbed texture roller

6 dowels

Ivory pearl trim

1 large, medium and small burgundy silk rose with leaves

9 pieces of green, artificial bear grass

Double-sided tape

Ivory ribbon for cake drum board

a

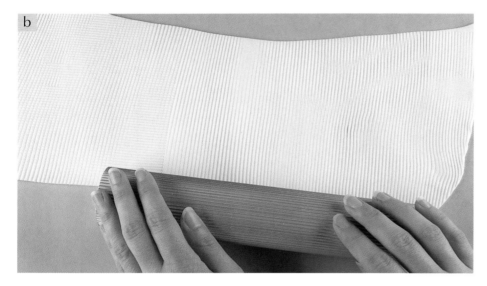

b

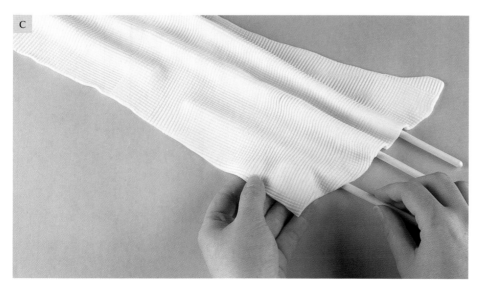

c

1 Place the oval cake onto the drum board, positioning it slightly towards the back. Cover the cake with marzipan (see page 19).

2 Cover the cake and board with ivory sugarpaste (see page 20). Crimp the edge of the paste on the board (pic a).

3 Put the round cake onto the thin cake board. Cover with marzipan (see page 19) and ivory sugarpaste (see page 20). Place the round cake on top of the oval cake, positioning it to the right. Secure in place with ivory-coloured royal icing. In this instance the bottom tier does not need to be dowelled as there is no weight in the top tier.

4 Roll out a strip of sugarpaste approximately 51 x 20cm (20 x 8in). Texture with the ribbed texture roller, first roll vertically and then horizontally (pic b).

5 Place the dowels onto your work surface so that you have three long rows – two dowels end to end in each row. Carefully place the sugarpaste strip over the dowels. Adjust the dowels if they move (pic c). Gently run your fingers up and down the sugarpaste-covered dowels so that you create three soft folds in the paste.

6 Remove the dowels. Loosely gather together one end of the strip, then carefully lift the sugarpaste strip into position on the cake. Put the gathered end onto the top cake and then drape the paste down from the top tier to the bottom (pic d). Trim the edges if needed.

7 Sterilize the ivory pearl trim (see Tip below). Add the trim around the base of each cake, securing with royal icing.

8 Arrange the roses and bear grass on the cakes and board and use royal icing to secure in position (pic e).

9 Stick double-sided tape around the cake drum board and trim with ivory ribbon.

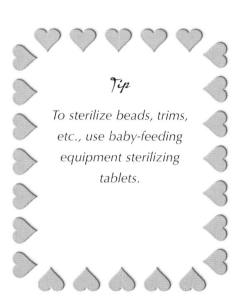

Tip

To sterilize beads, trims, etc., use baby-feeding equipment sterilizing tablets.

Rose Leaf
Cascade

This cake is covered in a cascade of rose leaves in shades of violet. You could, of course, use a different colour to match your wedding scheme.

Materials

15cm (6in), 20cm (8in) and 25cm (10in) round light fruit cakes (see page 11)

Apricot glaze

2.625kg (5lb 12oz) marzipan (see page 17)

500g (1lb 2oz) white sugarpaste (rolled fondant) (for the drum board)

800g (1lb 12oz) violet sugarpaste (rolled fondant)

220g (8oz) white sugarpaste (rolled fondant)

Clear alcohol or boiled water

60g (2¼oz) white flower paste (see page 17)

Violet dusting powder

Royal icing (see page 16)

Equipment

36cm (14in) round cake drum board

15cm (6in) and 20cm (8in) thin boards

Rolling pin

Sharp knife

Cake smoother

Closed vee serrated crimpers

12 dowels

Clingfilm (plastic wrap)

Veined rose leaf plunger cutters

Non-stick board

Set of leaf cutters

Flower former set

Dusting brush

Piping (decorating) bag fitted with a no. 2 piping tube (nozzle)

Small pieces of foam

Double-sided tape

Violet ribbon for the cake drum board

3 The cakes need to be supported with dowels. Follow the instructions on page 23 and then stack the cakes.

4 Prepare the sugarpaste for covering the cakes. Use approximately 600g (1lb 4oz) violet sugarpaste for the bottom tier. For the middle tier mix 100g (3½oz) of white and 150g (5oz) of violet. Finally, mix 120g (4¼oz) of white with 50g (2oz) of violet for the top tier. To prevent the paste from drying out, wrap each piece in clingfilm.

5 Roll out the sugarpaste for the bottom tier. Use the largest plunger cutter to cut out rose leaves. Press the plunger down onto the paste – this will vein the leaves. Remove the leaf shape from the cutter. (Pic a shows the three colours of paste and the three plunger cutters.) Dampen the marzipan on the side of the bottom tier with clear alcohol or boiled water and place a row of leaves around the bottom of the cake while they are still damp. About half of each leaf should sit on the board. Position the next row of leaves above the first row. The tip of the leaves should sit between the leaves on the first row (refer to the photo on page 51.) Work your way around the side of the bottom tier until it is covered (do not cover the top of the bottom tier cake).

6 Roll out the sugarpaste for the middle tier. Use the medium size plunger cutter to cut out the leaves in the same way as you did in step 5. Dampen the marzipan on the top of the bottom tier and side of the middle tier with clear alcohol or boiled water. Position the leaves on the top of the bottom tier cake and up the side of the middle tier until it is covered (do not cover the top of the middle tier).

7 Finally, use the sugarpaste for the top tier and the smallest plunger cutter and cut out the leaves. Position the leaves on the top of the middle tier, up the side of the top tier and then over the top until the cake is completely covered in leaves (pic b).

1 Place the largest cake centrally on the drum board. Place the other two cakes on the corresponding size thin boards. Cover the cakes with marzipan (see page 19).

2 Roll out the sugarpaste for the drum board into a strip approximately 114 x 8cm (45 x 3in) long. Dampen the base of the board with a little water then place the strip on it, around the cake. Overlap the ends and then trim. Work the two ends together so you cannot see the join. Smooth the paste with the cake smoother and trim off any excess. Crimp the edge of the paste.

8 Roll out the flower paste on a non-stick board. Cut out four large petals with the serrated edge cutter. Then, using the plain side of the medium cutter, cut out the centre of the large petals. Place into the large flower former to dry. Now cut out six medium-sized serrated petals and cut out the centres with the plain side of the small cutter. Place these in the medium former to dry. (Pic c.)

9 Dust the edges of all of the petals with violet dusting powder. Using royal icing, join two large petals together, base to base. Support the petals with small pieces of foam and leave to dry. Add the two remaining large petals as shown in pic d.

10 Place four of the medium-sized petals in the middle of the larger petals —the petals should curl downwards, through the centre of the larger petals. Secure in place with royal icing and allow to dry (pic e). Place the last two petals in the centre of the crown — the petals should curl upwards. Secure with royal icing and allow to dry.

11 When the crown is dry, position in the centre of the top tier of the cake, securing it with royal icing.

12 Stick double-sided tape around the cake drum board and trim with ribbon.

Tip

If you prefer you could use a different top-tier decoration. You could use a ready-made rose, or if you're feeling ambitious, try making your own sugarcraft rose.

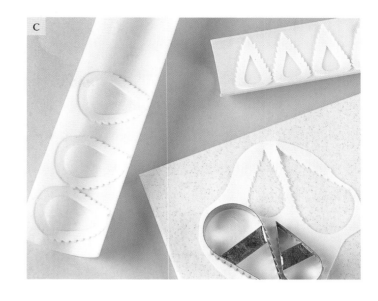

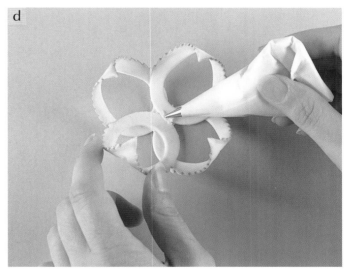

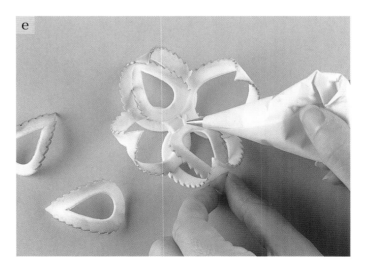

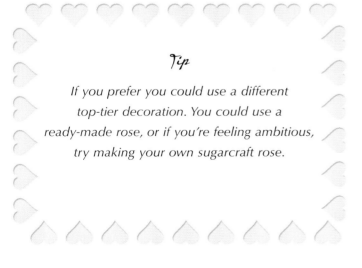

Chocolate
Delight

This cake is a dream-come-true for chocoholics — dark chocolate cigarellos and an abundance of chocolate hearts.

Materials

3 x 500g (1lb 2oz) boxes of dark chocolate cigarellos

3 deep hexagonal chocolate cakes – 10cm (4in), 15cm (6in) and 20cm (8in) point to point (see pages 12–13)

454g (1lb) jar of shredless orange marmalade

3 quantities of chocolate buttercream or ganache (see pages 15 and 18)

1.5kg (3lb 4oz) chocolate-flavoured sugarpaste (rolled fondant)

100 foil-wrapped chocolate hearts

Equipment

Heatproof bowl

Saucepan

25cm (10in) and 33cm (13in) flat to flat hexagonal cake drum boards

Sharp knife

Palette knife

10cm (4in) and 15cm (6in) flat to flat thin cake boards

Rolling pin

Cake smoother

12 dowels

Double-sided tape

Gold ribbon for cakes and drum boards

26g silver wire

Posy pick

1 Melt one or two cigarellos (see Tip on page 31). Make sure that neither water nor steam come into contact with the chocolate.

2 Fix the two drum boards together with a little melted chocolate. Cut the cakes in half horizontally and fill with marmalade. Place the largest cake centrally onto the drum boards with a little buttercream. Place the two other tiers on the appropriate thin cake boards in the same way.

3 Cover each cake with a layer of buttercream (pic a), then cover with sugarpaste (see page 20).

4 The cakes need to be supported with dowels, follow the instructions on page 23. Stack the cakes, making sure that each one is central.

5 Start placing the cigarellos around the bottom tier, using the melted chocolate to secure them in position. If your cake is deeper than the height of the cigarellos, place one row of cigarellos around the cake and then place another row of cigarellos above it. If necessary, use a warmed knife to cut the second row of cigarellos to the depth of the cake. Continue in the same way on the other two tiers (pic b).

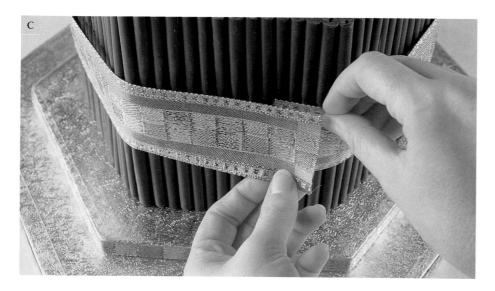

6 Stick double-sided tape around the two cake drum boards and trim with ribbon. Place a ribbon around the centre of each cake and secure at the back with double-sided tape (pic c).

7 Place the chocolate hearts on the drum boards and around the tops of the cakes.

8 Use the remaining hearts (you should have about 10 left) to make the top-tier decoration. Cut a length of wire for each chocolate heart (cut them in varying lengths). Taking great care, warm one end of each piece of wire (I use a cigarette lighter) and then push into the bottom of each heart (pic d). Allow to set (these are for decoration only and should not be eaten). Place a posy pick in the centre of the top cake. Put a little warmed chocolate into the pick then insert the wired hearts. Leave to set.

Glistening
Crystals

This cake is so elegant with its sparkling crystals glistening in the light and branches of delicate coloured gems. I have made the cake with four tiers, but of course you could use two or three if you prefer.

Materials
Royal icing (see page 16)

10cm (4in), 15cm (6in), 20cm (8in) and 25cm (10in) round rich fruit cakes (see page 12)

Apricot glaze

3.125kg (6lb 12oz) marzipan (see page 17)

Clear alcohol or boiled water

3.5kg (7lb 12oz) white sugarpaste (rolled fondant)

Equipment
33cm (13in) and 38cm (15in) round cake drum boards

Rolling pin

Sharp knife

Cake smoother

10cm (4in), 15cm (6in) and 20cm (8in) round thin cake boards

18 dowels

Double-sided tape

White ribbon for cake drum board

5m (16½ft) reel of clear iridescent diamond trim

Small piping (decorating) bag fitted with a no. 1.5 piping tube (nozzle)

Posy pick

8 large diamond-shaped crystals

26g silver wire

15 gem branches

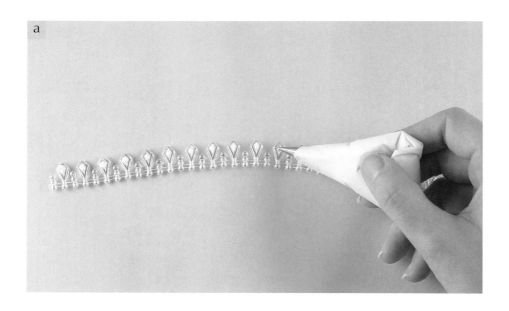

1 Fix the two drum boards together with a little royal icing. Allow to dry. Put the largest cake centrally onto the boards. Cover the cake with marzipan (see page 19). Place the other three tiers onto the appropriate size thin cake boards and cover each cake with marzipan.

2 Cover the largest cake and boards with sugarpaste. Cover the other cakes with sugarpaste. (See page 20).

3 The cakes need to be supported with dowels. Follow the instructions on page 23. Stack the cakes, making sure that they sit centrally on top of one another.

4 Run some double-sided tape around the bottom drum board and trim with ribbon. Run double-sided tape on top of the ribbon then edge with the diamond trim (the droplets should hang down). Measure around the smaller covered drum board and cut a piece of diamond trim to this length. Pipe a small dot of royal icing at the back of each diamond (pic a) and place onto the covered board.

5 Trim the base of each cake in the same way, but point the droplets upwards (pic b).

6 Pipe small dots of royal icing at random over each cake (pic c).

7 Insert a posy pick into the centre of the top tier (pic d). Thread the diamond-shaped crystals onto a short length of wire. Form the wire into a circle, bunching the crystals closely together (pic e). Twist the ends of the wire together. Place over the posy pick.

8 Arrange the gem branches in the posy pick.

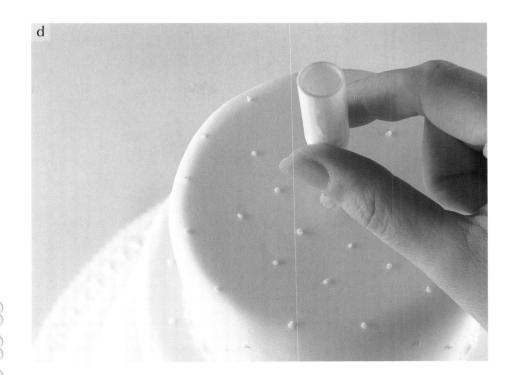

d

Tips

When using beads, crystals and trims like these it is advisable to sterilize them first before putting them on the cake. (See Tip on page 49.)

If the diamond-shaped crystals don't have a hole in the top to thread them, just place them onto the cake and fix in position with a little royal icing.

e

Coronet
and Cushions

These cushions hold the bride's coronet. Each cushion has a textured finish and is edged in gold frills. This cake would enhance any wedding table.

Materials

Clear alcohol or boiled water

3.5kg (7lb 12oz) ivory sugarpaste (rolled fondant)

25cm (10in) and 30cm (12in) square light or rich fruit cakes (see pages 11 and 12)

20cm (8in) square carrot cake (see page 14)

Apricot glaze

2.25kg (5lb) marzipan (see page 17)

1 quantity of buttercream (see page 14)

Cornflour (cornstarch)

75g (3oz) flower paste (see page 17)

Edible liquid gold

Royal icing (see page 16)

Equipment

41cm (16in) square cake drum board

Rolling pin

Sharp knife

Cake smoother

20cm (8in), 25cm (10in) and 30cm (12in) square thin cake boards

Palette knife

Rice, scroll and bubble texture rollers

12 dowels

Bead cutter

Ribbon cutter

Straight frill sets

Paintbrush

Piping (decorating) bag fitted with no. 1.5 piping tube (nozzle)

Double-sided tape

Gold ribbon for cake drum board

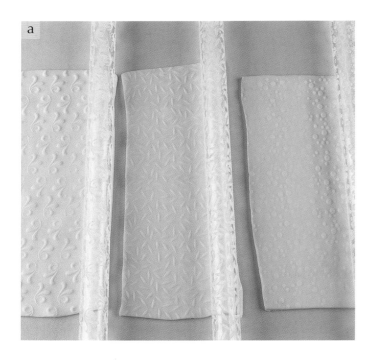

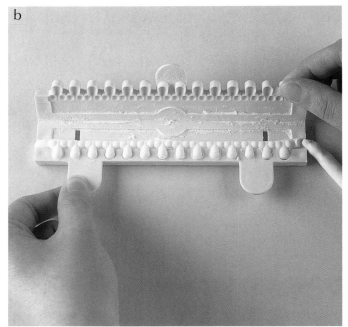

1 Dampen the drum board with clear alcohol or boiled water. Roll out 1kg (2lb 4oz) of sugarpaste and cover the board (see page 20). Keep any trimmings to use later.

2 Cut the cakes into cushion shapes (see cutting guide on page 65). Place each cake onto the appropriate sized thin cake board. Cover the fruit cakes with marzipan (see page 19) and coat the carrot cake with a layer of buttercream.

3 Roll out 600g (1lb 4oz) of sugarpaste for the carrot cake, the top tier. Texture with the rice texture roller. Cover the cake (see page 20). Gently pat the paste into position being careful not to rub off the textured pattern. Trim away any excess paste.

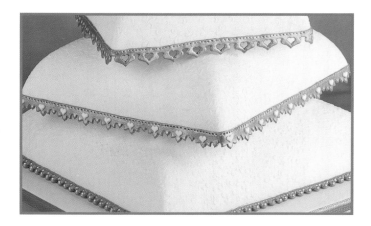

4 Use 750g (1lb 8oz) of sugarpaste for the middle tier. Roll out and texture with the scroll texture roller. Cover the cake. For the bottom tier, the largest cake, roll out 900g (2lb) of sugarpaste and texture with the bubble texture roller. Cover the cake. Leave all of the cakes to dry. (Pic a shows the effect achieved with all three textured rollers.)

5 The cakes need to be supported with dowels. Stack the cakes on the drum board, referring to the photograph on page 63 to position them correctly. Assess the area of each cake that needs to be dowelled and then follow the instructions on page 23.

6 Dust the bead cutter with cornflour. Mix 75g (3oz) of flower paste and 75g (3oz) of sugarpaste together. Roll into a sausage and place in the bead cutter. Close and press firmly together. Open (pic b) and trim the excess paste around the beads. You may find you need to go through this process a couple of times to get the best result. Gently lift the beads out of the bead cutter and place around the base of the bottom tier. Keep making beads until you have beads all around the base. Do not secure them to the cake at this stage. Leave to dry.

c

7 Roll out a strip of sugarpaste approximately 56 x 2cm (22 x ¾in). Use a ribbon cutter to trim to size. Cut one side of the strip with the no. 2 straight frill cutter. Place the strip around two sides of the middle tier. Secure with a little water. Repeat for the other two sides. Make any joins as neat as possible, blending the two ends together. Leave to dry.

8 Repeat step 7, but this time cut the strips to approximately 46 x 2cm (18 x ¾in) and cut with the no. 8 straight frill cutter (pic c). Remove the little hearts and set them aside for use later. Place the strip around two sides of the top tier. Secure with a little water. Repeat for the remaining two sides. Leave to dry.

9 Remove the beads from the base of the bottom tier and paint with edible liquid gold and leave to dry. When dry, place them back around the cake and secure with a little royal icing. Touch up any beads with the edible liquid gold as necessary.

Cutting guide

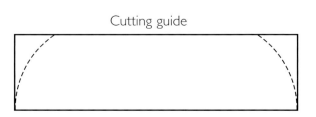

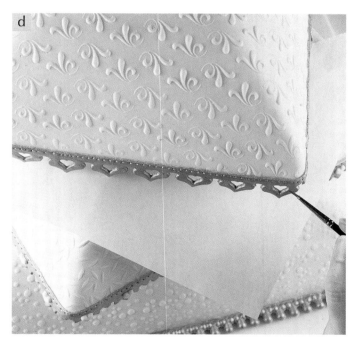

d

10 Paint the frills on the other two tiers with the edible liquid gold (pic d). Be careful not to get any gold on the ivory sugarpaste. Leave to dry. Add the little hearts (that you set aside in step 8) to the frill on the middle tier, securing them with royal icing.

11 Stick double-sided tape around the drum board and trim with ribbon.

Daisy *Daisy*

This modern, bright cake is so simple to make, yet so eye-catching.

You can change the colours of the flowers to match any

wedding scheme.

Materials

15cm (6in), 20cm (8in), 25cm (10in) and 30cm (12in) round madeira cakes (see page 13)

6 quantities of buttercream (see page 14)

Jam (jelly) optional

4.375kg (9lb 8oz) ivory sugarpaste (rolled fondant)

Cornflour (cornstarch)

250g (9oz) modelling paste (see page 18)

Paste colours: pink, white, yellow, ice blue, violet, tangerine

Clear alcohol

Royal icing (see page 16)

Equipment

40cm (15¾in) round cake drum board

15cm (6in), 20cm (8in) and 25cm (10in) thin round cake boards

Sharp knife

Palette knife

Rolling pin

Cake smoother

18 dowels

Piping (decorating) bag fitted with a no. 1.5 piping tube (nozzle)

Large daisy mould

Palette

Paintbrushes

Double-sided tape

Thin ribbon in colours to match daisies for cakes and drum board

1 Put the largest cake on the drum board and the other three cakes on the appropriate thin boards. Cut the cakes in half and fill with buttercream and jam if liked. Coat all four cakes with a layer of buttercream. Roll out the sugarpaste and cover the cakes and the drum board (see page 20).

2 The cakes need to be supported with dowels (see page 23). Stack the cakes. Add a little cooled, boiled water to a small amount of sugarpaste and mix until a piping consistency is achieved. Put in the piping bag and fill the joins between the tiers. Smooth the joins and leave to dry.

3 Dust the daisy mould with cornflour and push a small amount of modelling paste into the mould. Trim any excess paste. Lift the daisy out of the mould (pic a); trim if necessary. Leave to dry. Make approximately 39 daisies.

4 Paint the daisies using the paste colours, thinned with a little clear alcohol (pic b). You will need seven in each colour (this allows for mishaps). Use yellow for all of the flower centres except for the yellow daisies; for these use tangerine. Mix white with the pink, violet and blue paste colours as they are very strong. Paint the back of the daisies too.

5 Set aside the painted daisies to dry.

6 Once dry set aside three different coloured daisies for the top decoration. Position the rest of the daisies on the cake, spacing them evenly around the side of each tier and alternating the colours. Secure in place with royal icing (pic c).

7 Stand three daises on top of the cake and secure with royal icing (pic d).

8 Stick double-sided tape around the drum board and trim with different coloured ribbons. Place a ribbon around each tier and secure the ends with double-sided tape (pic e).

Tip

The brightly coloured daisies give this cake a modern, funky feel. However if you wanted to, you could take the basic idea of this design but use different flowers and colours to create a cake with a very different feel.

Christmas
Rose Collar

This is a very traditional cake with collars, flowers and pillars.

Materials

10cm (6in) and 23cm (9in) point to point, hexagonal rich fruit cakes (see page 12)

Apricot glaze

1.375kg (2lb 12oz) marzipan (see page 17)

Clear alcohol or boiled water

1.75kg (3lb 12oz) white sugarpaste (rolled fondant)

Royal icing (see page 16)

Flower paste (see page 17)

Dusting powders: snowflake, lemon ice, frosty holly

Edible glue

Equipment

20cm (8in) and 30cm (12in) flat to flat, hexagonal cake drum boards

Rolling pin

Sharp knife

Cake smoother

Closed vee serrated crimpers

Diamond side design

Double-sided tape

Fine gold bead trim

Piping (decorating) bag fitted with a no. 2 piping tube (nozzle)

White ribbon for drum boards

Non-stick board

Christmas rose corner cutter

Paintbrush

Veining board

Christmas rose cutter

Ball tool

Petal veining mat

26g white floral wire

240 mini double-ended lemon yellow stamens

Pale green florist's tape

3 white pillars, 7.5cm (3in) tall and 3 dowels

1 Place the 10cm (6in) cake on the 20cm (8in) board and the 23cm (9in) cake on the 30cm (12in) board. Cover the cakes with marzipan (see page 17). Cover the cakes and boards with sugarpaste (see page 20). Crimp the edges of the paste on the board.

2 Use the diamond side design to emboss around the sides of the cakes. Emboss a single droplet in the top point of each diamond (pic a).

3 Place gold bead trim around the base of each cake and secure with royal icing.

4 Stick double-sided tape around the edge of the boards and trim with ribbon. Run a thin piece of double-sided tape around the centre of the ribbon and place the gold bead trim on it.

5 Roll out flower paste on a non-stick board. Use the corner cutter to cut out six corners for each cake (pic b). Carefully cut off the side leaves on six of the corners; these are for the top tier. Place on a flat surface to dry.

6 Mix a little clear alcohol with each dusting powder. Paint the petals with snowflake, the flower centres with lemon ice and the leaves with frosty holly. Leave to dry.

Tip

Keep this cake in a dry, cool place as you do not want the collars to droop.

7 Roll out flower paste on the veining board. Cut out 15 large and 15 medium petals using the Christmas rose cutter (pic c). Ball the outer edges of the petals, then vein with the petal veining mat. Cut fifteen 4cm (1½in) lengths of florist's wire and push into the vein in the back of each petal. Secure the wire with edible glue. Leave to dry.

8 Fold 40 stamens in half and use the florist's tape to tape to a short length of wire. Tape five medium petals around the stamens (pic d). Trim the wires to 2.5cm (1in). This is a complete flower. Make five medium flowers and five large flowers in this way.

9 Place the Christmas rose corners onto the cake; they sit at each point of the hexagon. (Remember that the corners without the side leaves are for the top tier.) Secure with a little royal icing (pic e).

10 To position the pillars on the bottom tier, follow the instructions on pages 21–22. Place the large flowers centrally on the bottom tier and secure with royal icing. Put the top tier in position, place the medium flowers in the middle and secure.

Lace and *Hydrangeas*

This is a very stylish wedding cake.

Materials

10cm (4in), 20cm (8in) and 25cm (10in) round rich fruit cakes (see page 12)

Apricot glaze

2.5kg (5lb 8oz) marzipan (see page 17)

Clear alcohol or boiled water

3kg (6lb 8oz) white sugarpaste (rolled fondant)

Royal icing (see page 16)

200g (7oz) flower paste

Cornflour (cornstarch)

White vegetable fat

Edible glue

Violet dusting powder

Spruce green paste colour

Confectioner's varnish

Equipment

33cm (13in) cake drum board

10cm (4in) and 20cm (8in) round thin cake boards

Rolling pin

Sharp knife

Cake smoother

Triple serrated crimpers

Piping bag fitted with a no 1.5 piping tube (nozzle)

10cm (4in) diameter candle holder

2 non-stick boards

Chantilly, Austrian, lily lace cutters

Paintbrush

Scriber

14 small pieces of foam or small jar lids

Double-sided tape

White ribbon for cake drum board

12 dowels

26g white floral wire

Veining board

Small Christmas rose cutter

Ball tool

Pale green florist's tape

Small leaf cutter

Camellia leaf veiner

Posy pick

1 Put the largest cake centrally onto the drum board. Put the other two cakes on the appropriate size thin boards. Cover the cakes with marzipan (see page 17). Cover the largest cake and board with sugarpaste. Crimp the edge of the board. Use royal icing to pipe a snail trail around the base of the cake (see Tip on page 80). Cover the other two cakes with sugarpaste. Wash the candle holder and place the small cake onto it.

2 Roll out the flower paste on a non-stick board, to a thickness of approximately 2mm (⅛in). Dust the lily lace cutter with cornflour. Press the cutter down onto the paste, twist, then rotate in a circular motion. Lift the cutter away from the paste. Smear a second non-stick board with white vegetable fat. Place the cutter down onto the fat, pause until you feel a slight suction, then lift the cutter away to leave the lace cutout on the board (pic a shows the three different lace cutters and lace pieces). Lift out the inner lace pieces with a scriber. Cut a further 10 pieces of lace in the same way. Lift the lace pieces with a sharp knife and place around the base of the small cake (pic b), securing with a little water.

3 To cut the lace for the middle tier use the Austrian lace cutter. You will need 10 pieces of lace. Cut the lace pieces as described in step 2, again removing the inner pieces of paste. Place around the base of the middle tier, securing with a little water.

a

b

4 For the lace pieces for the bottom tier use the Chantilly lace cutter. You will need 28 pieces. (You do not need to remove the inner lace pieces.) Leave the lace pieces to dry on a flat surface.

5 Space 14 Chantilly lace pieces evenly around the board — the lace pieces stand on the board and "lean" against the cake at a 45-degree angle. Secure in place to the board and the cake with a small dot of royal icing.

6 The other 14 pieces of Chantilly lace are positioned on the side of the cake, but slightly higher, in between the pieces already in place. Position each piece at a 45-degree angle, securing in place with royal icing. Support with foam or small jar lids (pic c). Leave to dry.

7 Stick double-sided tape around the drum board and trim with ribbon.

8 The cakes need to be supported with dowels. Follow the instructions on page 23. Stack the cakes.

9 Cut 56 10cm (4in) lengths of floral wire. Add a small ball of flower paste to each wire and secure with edible glue. Work the ball down the wire to make a stamen shape and mark a cross on the top. (Pic d shows the flower heads in the making, the completed hydrangea and the table decoration.)

c

10 Roll out the flower paste on a veining board. Use the Christmas rose cutter to cut out 224 petals (each flower head is made up of four petals). Ball the outer edges of the petals using the ball tool, then insert a short wire in the back of each petal. Leave to dry.

11 Dust the petals and flower head centres with violet dusting powder.

12 Tape four petals around a stamen to form a flower head. Repeat to make 56 flower heads (you will use about 50 to complete the hydrangea, keep the others for use later). Tape the flower heads together into groups of three. Add one group of three together, then add another and so on, until you have a nice rounded hydrangea.

13 Colour a small amount of flower paste with spruce green. Roll out on the veining board. Using the serrated edge of the small leaf cutter, cut out seven leaves. Ball the edge of the leaves then insert a 10cm (4in) length of wire in the back of each leaf. Vein the leaves with the camellia veiner and leave to dry.

14 Paint the leaves with spruce green to get a darker green colour. Leave to dry. Brush the leaves with confectioner's varnish.

15 Place a posy pick in the top tier. Put five leaves in the posy pick and bend the wires so that the leaves lay on top of the cake. Place the hydrangea in the posy pick.

16 Group the remaining flower heads into two groups of three. Tape each group and cut the wires to 2.5cm (1in). Position one group on top of the middle tier and secure with royal icing. Tape two leaves to the other group and place at the front of the cake on the table.

d

Ivory and *Mint Triangles*

This cake has a "Wedgwood" look to it, with its simple, flowing design.

Materials

20cm (8in), 25cm (10in) and 30cm (12in) triangular light fruit cakes (see page 11)

Apricot glaze

3.875kg (8lb 8oz) marzipan (see page 17)

3.875kg (8lb 8oz) white sugarpaste (rolled fondant)

Paste colours: mint green, ivory

Clear alcohol or boiled water

Royal icing (see page 16)

Cornflour (cornstarch)

Ivory-coloured flower paste (see page 17)

Edible glue

Equipment

30cm (12in), 36cm (14in) and 46cm (18in) triangular cake drum boards

Rolling pin

Sharp knife

Cake smoother

Closed scallop serrated crimpers

Piping (decorating) bag fitted with no. 1.5 piping tube (nozzle)

Non-stick board

Lace flower cutter

Veining board

Lace leaf set

26g white floral wire

Small pieces of foam

45 small double-ended stamens

9 medium double-ended stamens

White florist's tape

Ball tool

Large blossom veiner

Flower former

Double-sided tape

Ivory ribbon for drum boards

3-tier "E" stand

1 Place each cake on the appropriate board. Cover the cakes with marzipan (see page 19). Colour the white sugarpaste with the mint green paste colour. Cover the cakes and boards with the mint green sugarpaste (see page 20). Crimp the edges of the paste on the boards.

2 Colour a little royal icing with ivory paste colour to match the flower paste. Use the paste colour a little at a time as most colours deepen as they dry. Put the royal icing in the piping bag and pipe a snail trail (see Tip below) around the base of each cake.

a

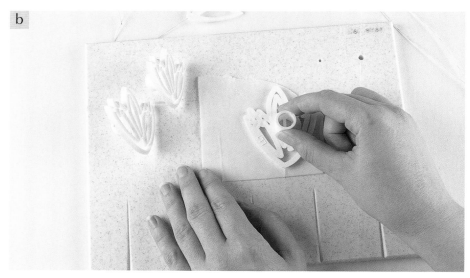

b

Tip

To pipe a snail trail hold the tube slightly above the surface you are piping on. Squeeze the bag, letting the icing out into a ball shape. Gradually relax the pressure and draw the tube down to the surface. This will give you a small ball with a tail.

3 Dust a non-stick board with cornflour and on it roll out some flower paste. Cut out 21 lace flowers, nine for the bottom tier and six each for the other two tiers (pic a). Press the cutter firmly into the paste. Position the lace flowers onto the cakes while the paste is still soft. On the top and bottom tiers place the first flower squarely on one of the sides, continue around the cakes. On the middle tier place the first flower over the front point of the triangle, continue around the cake.

4 Roll out some flower paste on a veining board. Cut out three leaves using the largest lace leaf cutter (pic b). Cut three 8cm (3in) lengths of white floral wire. Insert a wire into the base of each leaf through the groove. Leave to dry on small pieces of foam, propping up some of the edges so that when they dry the leaves will be shaped and look as though they have some movement in them. Repeat this with the next two largest cutters in the set. This will give you nine leaves in total.

5 Cut nine 8cm (3in) lengths of white floral wire. Take five small double-ended stamens and fold them in half. Place one slightly larger stamen with them and tape onto a length of wire. Make nine of these.

6 Roll out some flower paste on a non-stick board. Cut out three of each size blossom using the templates on page 110 (pic c). Ball the outer edge of the petals, then vein in the blossom veiner (pic d). Place a little edible glue in the centre of each blossom and push the wired stamens in place. Put in a flower former to dry.

7 Tape the three large blossoms together and add the largest lace leaves in between the blossoms. Do the same with the medium and small blossoms and leaves. Place the large leaves and blossoms on the bottom tier, the medium leaves and blossoms on the middle tier and finally the small leaves and blossoms on the top tier (pic e). Secure with a little royal icing.

8 Stick double-sided tape around the drum boards and trim with ribbon. Place the cakes on the stand.

c

d

e

White
Wedding

This is a traditional wedding cake using pillars to form the tiers. Whilst the result is very impressive, this cake is very simple to make as the sugarflower sprays are bought ready-made.

Materials

15cm (6in), 20cm (8in) and 25cm (10in) petal-shaped light or rich fruit cakes (see pages 11 and 12)

Apricot glaze

2.5kg (5lb 8oz) marzipan (see page 17)

Clear alcohol or boiled water

2.5kg (5lb 8oz) white sugarpaste (rolled fondant)

Royal icing (see page 16)

Equipment

20cm (8in), 25cm (10in) and 33cm (13in) petal-shaped cake drum boards

Rolling pin

Sharp knife

Cake smoother

Closed scallop serrated crimpers

White pearl trim

Piping (decorating) bag fitted with no. 1.5 piping tube (nozzle)

Double-sided tape

White ribbon for cake drum board

6 round pillars, 9cm (3½in) tall

6 dowels

Large, medium and small white sugarcraft rose sprays

Bride and groom (optional)

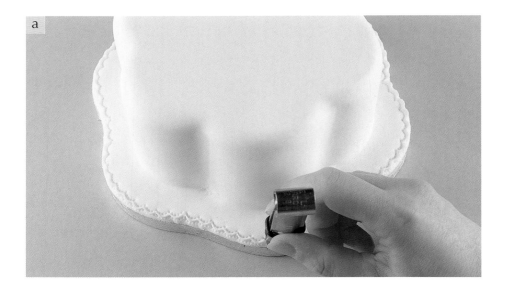

a

1 Place each cake on the appropriate board. Cover the cakes with marzipan (see page 19). Cover the cakes and boards with white sugarpaste (see page 20). Crimp the edge of the paste on the board (pic a).

2 Sterilize the pearl trim (see Tip page 49) and place it around the base of each cake and secure with royal icing (pic b).

3 Stick double-sided tape around each drum board and trim with ribbon.

b

Tip

There are many different styles and designs of bride and groom decoration. Have a look around as you're sure to find one that you like.

c

d

4 Follow the instructions on pages 21–23 for assembling a cake with pillars (pic c). Stack the cakes.

5 Arrange the rose sprays on the cakes – the large spray on the largest cake and so on (pic d). Secure in position with royal icing. Place a bride and groom decoration on the top tier if liked. Secure in position with royal icing.

Pink
Bubbles

Pink is a very popular wedding colour and this cake is a modern take on the traditional pastel pink cake. This cake is stylish but lots of fun.

Materials

15cm (6in), 20cm (8in) and 25cm (10in) rich fruit cakes (see page 12)

Apricot glaze

2.625kg (12oz) marzipan (see page 17)

Clear alcohol or boiled water

3kg (6lb 8oz) shell pink sugarpaste (rolled fondant)

Equipment

36cm (14in) round cake drum board

15cm (6in) and 20cm (8in) round thin cake boards

Rolling pin

Sharp knife

Cake smoother

Closed curve serrated crimpers

12 dowels

Piping (decorating) bag fitted with no. 1.5 piping tube (nozzle)

150cm (59in) pink wired ribbon

4m (79in) pink beaded wire

26g gold wire

Pink beads

Small, clear candleholder

Assortment of food-safe feathers

Double-sided tape

Pale pink ribbon

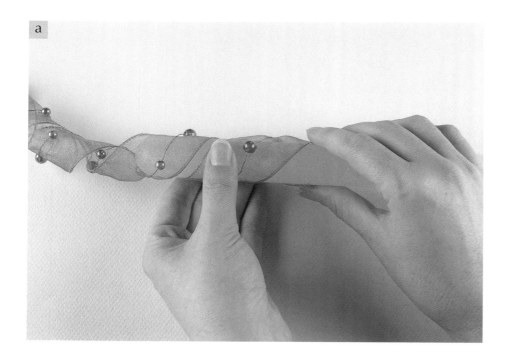

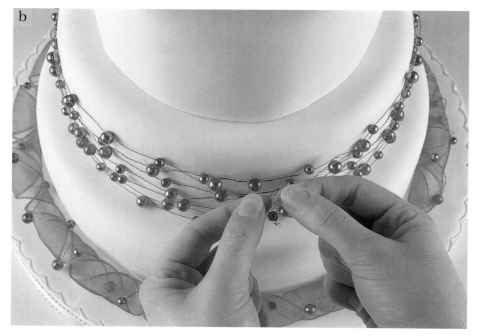

1 Put the largest cake centrally on the drum board and the other two cakes on the appropriate thin boards. Cover the cakes with marzipan (see page 19). Using pink sugarpaste, cover the largest cake and drum board in one (see page 20). While the paste is still soft, crimp the edge of the paste on the board.

2 Cover the other two cakes with pink sugarpaste (see page 20).

3 The cakes need to be supported with dowels. Follow the instructions on page 23. Stack the cakes. Add a little cooled, boiled water to a small amount of the pink sugarpaste and mix until you achieve a piping consistency. Put into the piping bag and pipe around the bases of the two top tiers to fill in the joins. Carefully smooth the icing with your little finger.

4 Wind the wired ribbon and then 150cm (59in) of the pink beaded wire around a rolling pin to form soft curls (pic a). Take off the rolling pin and place around the base of the bottom tier; twist the ends of the wires together to secure.

5 Measure around the middle tier and add 5cm (2in). Cut about seven lengths of the pink beaded wire to this length. Wrap each length of wire around the cake, one above the other, twisting the ends of the wire together to secure (pic b).

Tip

When using beads or trims it is advisable to sterilize them first before putting them on the cake (see Tip on page 49).

6 Cut two 31.5cm (1ft) lengths of gold wire. Join the ends of the wires together to make one long length. Thread a pink bead onto the wire, pushing it to the middle. Bend the wire down either side of the bead and then twist underneath the bead to secure. Thread six more beads onto the length of wire, spacing them 25mm (1in) apart (pic c). Twist the wire either side of each bead to hold it in place. Make about nine of these.

7 Fill the candleholder with pink beads. Arrange the beaded wires that you made in step 6 and the feathers in the candle-holder (pic d). Place onto the top of the cake.

8 Using the remaining pink beaded wire, form it into a zig-zag. Wind around the base of the candleholder.

9 Stick double-sided tape around the edge of the drum board and trim with ribbon.

c

d

Tip

You could fill the candleholder with sweets (candy) instead of beads and replace the feathers with artificial flowers.

Pretty
in Pink

This cake would appeal to most with its pretty shades of pink and fun feathers. This cake design would also work very well in black and white.

Materials

15cm (6in) round, 25cm (10in) petal and 30cm (12in) round rich fruit cakes (see page 12)

Apricot glaze

3.375kg (7lb 8oz) marzipan (see page 17)

Clear alcohol or boiled water

2kg (4lb 8oz) pink sugarpaste (rolled fondant) for 30cm (12in) round cake

1.25kg (2lb 12oz) shell pink sugarpaste for 25cm (10in) petal cake

500g (1lb 2oz) white sugarpaste for 15cm (6in) round cake

250g (9oz) deep pink sugarpaste for decoration

Edible glue

Equipment

36cm (14in) round cake drum board

25cm (10in) petal thin cake board

15cm (6in) round thin cake board

Rolling pin

Sharp knife

Cake smoother

Closed triple scallop serrated crimpers

12 dowels

Fancy button with embossed design

Circle cutters

Leaf scroll cutter

Lace strip embossers

Cutting wheel

Textured lace heart cutter

10 food-safe pink fluffy feathers

26g white wire

Posy pick

Double-sided tape

Dark pink ribbon for cake drum board

1 Place the 30cm (12in) round cake centrally onto the drum board. Place the other tiers on the appropriate thin boards. Cover the cakes with marzipan (see page 19). Cover the large round fruit cake and board in one with pink sugarpaste (see page 20). While the paste is still soft, crimp the edge of the paste on the drum board.

2 Cover the petal cake with the shell pink sugarpaste and the small round cake with white sugarpaste. (Keep all the trimmings as you will need them for making the decoration.)

3 The cakes need to be supported with dowels. Follow the instructions on page 23. Stack the cakes.

4 Roll out some shell pink sugarpaste. Use a clean, fancy button to emboss the paste. Cut around the embossed pattern with a circle cutter. Make six of these. To put them on the bottom tier use the petal cake above as a guide. Where the petal cake cuts in, follow the line down and place the embossed circle in that position. Secure with edible glue. Cut out six leaf scrolls and place them in between the circles. (Pic a.)

5 Roll out a thin strip of shell pink sugarpaste 89 x 2cm (35 x ¾in). Use the lace strips to emboss a narrow lace strip and cut out with the cutting wheel. Place around the base of the petal cake, securing with edible glue.

6 Roll out some pink sugarpaste. Using the textured lace heart cutter, cut out three lace hearts (pic b). Place around the side of the middle tier on every other petal.

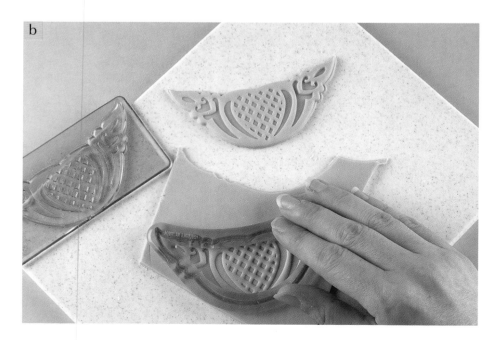

7 Roll out the deep pink sugarpaste into a strip approximately 36 × 15cm (14 × 6in). Use the lace strips to emboss three border lace strips and three narrow lace strips (pic c). Cut out with the cutting wheel. Referring to the photo on page 91, place the border strips over the top and down the sides of the top tier; secure in place with edible glue. Then do the same with the narrower strips, placing them in between the border strips.

8 Wire the fluffy pink feathers together (pic d). Place a posy pick into the top of the top tier and arrange the feathers in it. The feathers should not come into contact with the top of the cake.

9 Stick double-sided tape around the drum board and trim with ribbon.

Tip

You could use beaded wires or artificial flowers in the top of the cake instead of feathers.

Regal
Elegance

This very formal cake has majestic side decoration highlighted with shimmering dust and is softened with fresh, fragrant flowers.

Materials

15cm (6in), 20cm (8in), 25cm (10in) and 30cm (12in) round rich fruit cakes (see page 12)

Apricot glaze

4.25kg (9lb 4oz) marzipan (see page 17)

Clear alcohol or boiled water

4.5kg (10lb) white sugarpaste (rolled fondant)

1 quantity modelling paste (see page 18)

Royal icing (see page 16)

Pearl white dust

Equipment

20cm (8in), 25cm (10in), 30cm (12in) and 38cm (15in) round cake drum boards

Rolling pin

Sharp knife

Cake smoother

Closed triple scallop plain crimpers

Non-stick board

Creative plaque cutters set

Formers

Piping (decorating) bag fitted with no. 2 piping tube (nozzle)

18 dowels

4 round pieces of oasis, 7.5 x 6.5cm deep (3 x 2½in deep)

4 flower holders

Ruler

Greaseproof paper

Fresh flowers (see Tips on page 41)

Double-sided tape

Ivory ribbon for cake drum boards

Bride and groom decoration (optional)

1 Put the cakes centrally on the appropriate drum boards – each cake sits on the board that is slightly larger than it. Cover the cakes with marzipan (see page 19). Cover all of the cakes and boards in one with white sugarpaste (see page 20). Crimp the edges of the paste on the boards.

2 Roll out the modelling paste on a non-stick board. Use the creative plaque cutters with the raised trellis embosser set inside to cut out the side pieces. The plaque cutters come in four sizes so start with smallest cutter for the smallest cake, then the next size cutter for the 20cm (8in) cake and so on. You will need 12 side pieces for the 15cm (6in) cake, 14 for the 20cm (8in) cake, 16 for the 25cm (10in) cake and 18 for the 30cm (12in) cake. Emboss each one by pressing the plunger. Remove the paste from the cutter and dust with pearl white lustre. Place onto the formers to dry (pic a).

3 Evenly space the side pieces around each of the cakes, securing with royal icing (pic b).

4 The cakes need to be supported with dowels. Mark the positions for the dowels on the bottom tier (see page 23). Put a piece of dry oasis into a flower holder and place in the centre of the cake. Push a dowel into the cake. Place a ruler (or other straight edge) flat on top of the oasis and in line with the dowel. Make a mark where the ruler touches the dowel. Take the dowel out of the cake and cut where you made the mark. All of the dowels need to be cut to this length (pic c). You will need six dowels in each of the first two tiers and four in the third tier.

5 Cut a circle of greaseproof paper for each cake. The circles should be 25mm (1in) less in diameter than the top of the cake. These circles will be placed on top of the cakes so that the flowers do not sit directly on them. Also, use them as a guide for cutting the flowers to the appropriate length.

6 On the morning of the wedding, put soaked oasis into the flower holders. For the first, second and third tiers place the flowers around the side of the oasis (pic d). To achieve the rounded posy arrangement for the top tier place flowers around the side of the oasis and then build up the arrangement over the top of the oasis.

7 Stick double-sided tape around the drum boards and trim with ribbon. To stack the cakes place the largest circle of greaseproof paper on the bottom tier, pushing it over the dowels, then put the flowers for that tier in place. Continue in this way, stacking the cakes and put the posy arrangement on the top tier. Place the bride and groom decoration next to the cake.

Tip

Soak the oasis in water overnight.

Frills, Flowers
and Pearls

Soft frills of sugarpaste are decorated with pearls and a large carnation on this sophisticated, single-tier design. This is a very unusual, beautiful cake, perfect for a small, informal wedding.

Materials

18cm (7in) round light fruit cake (see page 11)

Apricot glaze

750g (1lb 8oz) marzipan (see page 17)

Clear alcohol or boiled water

1.25kg (2lb 12oz) ivory sugarpaste (rolled fondant)

Ivory flower paste (see page 17)

Pearl ivory lustre

Edible glue

Equipment

28cm (11in) round cake drum board

Rolling pin

Sharp knife

Cake smoother

Fabric texture roller

Ribbon cutter

Endless garret frill cutter

Bulbous cone tool

Bead cutter

Paintbrush

Non-stick board

Round garret frill cutter

Double-sided tape

Ivory ribbon for cake drum board

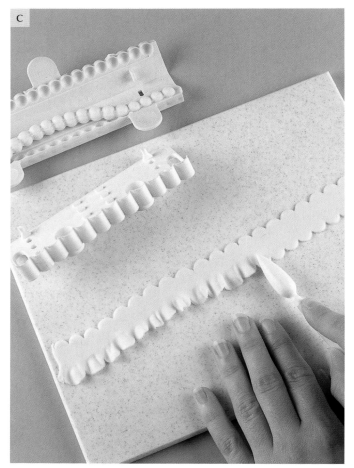

1   Place the cake onto the drum board. Brush the cake with apricot glaze and cover with marzipan (see page 19).

2   Roll out a strip of ivory sugarpaste approximately 89 x 13cm (35 x 5in). Dampen the base of the drum board with a little water, then place the strip around the board. Overlap the ends of the sugarpaste strip, then trim. Work the two ends together so you cannot see the join. Smooth the paste with a cake smoother and trim off the excess paste around the edge of the board. Texture the paste with the fabric texture roller (pic a).

3   Brush the marzipan with clear alcohol or boiled water. Roll out a long strip of ivory sugarpaste, approximately 61 x 5cm (2ft x 2in) using the ribbon cutter. Fold the strip lengthwise, but do not press the fold, keep it rounded. Place onto the cake starting at the base with the rounded fold at the bottom (pic b) and wind the strip around once. Neatly trim the end. Repeat until the cake is completely covered. Decrease the size of the strip as you go on to the top of the cake. You should end up with a small circle – fill this with a small spiral of paste (refer to photo on page 99).

4   Measure from the top centre of the cake down to the drum board. Cut a strip of ivory sugarpaste to this length, and approximately 3cm (1⅛in) wide. Using an endless garret frill cutter, cut a scalloped edge each side of the strip. Use a bulbous cone tool to fill the edges (pic c) then place onto the cake from the centre top to the drum board and secure with edible glue.

5 Mix 20g (¾oz) of flower paste with the same amount of ivory sugarpaste. Dust the bead cutter with pearl ivory lustre, then roll a sausage and place it across the length of the bead cutter. Close the bead cutter, pressing it firmly together. Open and trim the excess paste around the beads. You may find that you need to do this a couple of times to get nice rounded beads (pic c).

6 Gently lift the beads out of the bead cutter and place down the centre of the frill. Secure with edible glue (pic d).

7 Roll out flower paste on a non-stick board. Use the round garret frill cutter to make the large carnation (pic e). Start with the centre; cut the first piece out then fill with the bulbous cone tool. Fold it in half, then bring one third up to the centre, then take the other third to the centre in the opposite direction, this should look like an S-shape. Pinch the base together. Cut out about 8 more petals, fill with the bulbous cone tool and place these onto the centre, securing with edible glue. The first few petals will need to be squeezed around the bottom of the centre, but as the flower builds you should leave the petals more open. When complete place on top of the cake and secure with edible glue.

8 Stick double-sided tape around the edge of the drum board and trim with ivory ribbon.

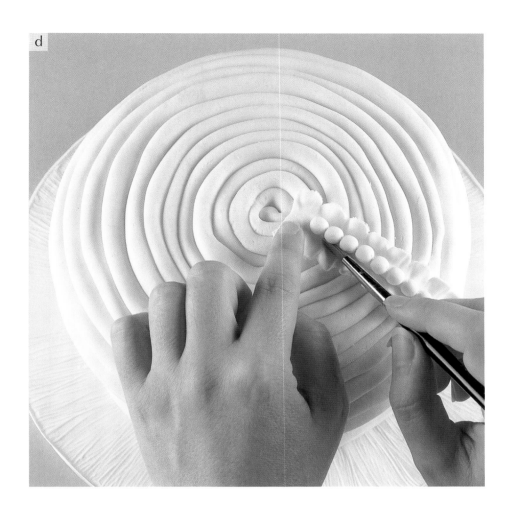

Swags
and Roses

Pretty rainbow-coloured ribbon roses are paired with elegant swags.

This cake would be perfect for a spring or summer wedding. It would be

particularly lovely for a reception in a garden.

Materials

15cm (6in) and 25cm (10in) round madeira cakes
(see page 13)

Jam (jelly) optional

3 quantities of buttercream (see page 14)

1.75kg (3lb 12oz) white sugarpaste (rolled fondant) for
covering cakes and boards

1kg (2lb 4oz) white sugarpaste for the decorations

Royal icing (see page 16)

Paste colours: pink, baby blue, violet, yellow, peach,
mint green

Equipment

Sharp knife

Palette knife

20cm (8in) and 33cm (13in) round cake drum boards

Cake smoother

Rolling pin

Closed curve serrated crimpers

9 scourers or dowels

Piping (decorating) bag fitted with a no. 2
piping tube (nozzle)

Ribbon cutter

Veined rose leaf plunger, 31mm (1¼in)

Double-sided tape

Ivory ribbon for cake drum boards

2-tier "C" stand

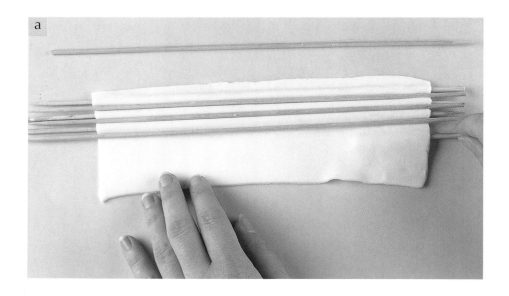

a

1 Cut the cakes in half horizontally and fill with jam and buttercream if liked. Place the 15cm (6in) cake on the 20cm (8in) board and the 25cm (10in) cake on the 33cm (13in) board. Cover the cakes with a layer of buttercream. Cover the cakes and boards in one with white sugarpaste (see page 20). Crimp the edge of the paste around the board.

2 Divide each cake equally into four – imagine the top of the cake as a clock face and make a little mark at the outer edge of the cake at 12, 3, 6 and 9 o'clock. This is a guide for placing the swags. Measure the distance between the marks then add about 5cm (2in) to that length. Roll out a piece of sugarpaste to that length and 6cm (2½in) wide.

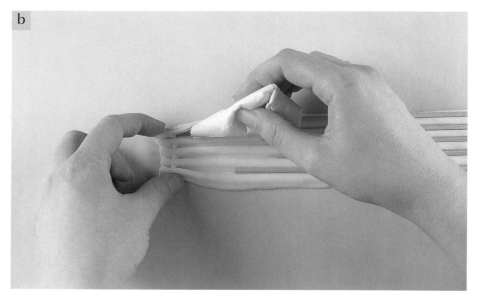

b

3 Place one scourer underneath the paste and then place another next to it, but on top of the paste this time. Continue in this way until you have placed the nine scourers (pic a).

4 Draw back the scourers slightly and add a little dot of royal icing at one end of the strip, in each fold. Remove the scourers completely and repeat at the other end (pic b). Take one end in each hand and pinch the folds together.

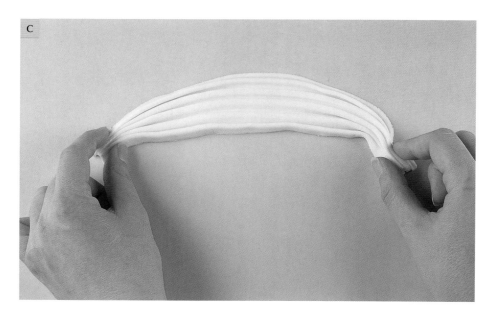

c

5 Curve the swag (pic c). Put some royal icing at the top of the side of the cake where you have made the marks. Pick the swag up by the two ends and place onto the cake, each end should sit on a mark; you will need to hold in

position for a few minutes. When securely in place trim the ends. You will need to make and position four swags for each cake.

6 Roll out four 4 x 4cm (1½ x 1½in) squares of sugarpaste, these will form the centre of the swags. Using seven scourers, follow the instructions in steps 3 and 4. Make four centres and place them over the joins of the swags. Secure with royal icing.

7 Make six 50g (2oz) balls of sugarpaste. Colour each ball with one of the paste colours. Roll out all of the coloured pastes except for the mint green. Use the ribbon cutter set at 35mm (1½in) wide to cut out a strip at least 8cm (3in) long. Loosely fold this in half lengthways and simply roll it to form a ribbon rose (pic d). When complete, trim the bottom flat with a sharp knife. You will need 36 roses for the bottom tier, 15 for the top tier and 8 for the sides of the cakes. Leave to dry.

8 Roll out the mint green sugarpaste and cut out 40 rose leaves, veining them by pressing the plunger on the cutter. You will need approximately 16 leaves for the bottom tier, 8 for the top tier and 16 for the sides of the cakes.

9 Take a small amount of white sugarpaste and make two small dome shapes – one 5cm (2in) in diameter (for the bottom tier), the other 10cm (4in) in diameter (for the top tier). Arrange the roses on top of the domes, securing them

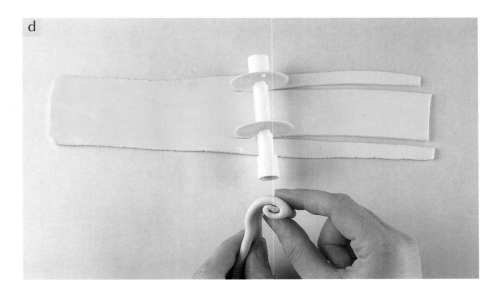

with royal icing (pic e). When complete, place the largest rose posy on the bottom tier and the smaller posy on the top tier. Arrange the leaves around the rose posies, securing them all with royal icing. Place a single rose with a leaf either side at the base of the cake in line with the centre of each swag.

10 Stick double sided tape around the edge of the cake drum boards and trim with ribbon.

11 Place the cakes on the stand.

Victoriana
Flower and Lace

This cake was inspired by a Victorian lace pattern, a simple, classic look. There are many different lace moulds available.

Materials

Two 20cm (8in) teardrop light fruit cakes (see page 11)

20cm (8in) heart-shaped madeira cake (see page 13)

Apricot glaze

1kg (2lb 4oz) marzipan (see page 17)

Clear alcohol or boiled water

1 quantity of buttercream (see page 14)

2.25kg (5lb) white sugarpaste (rolled fondant) for the cakes and decoration

1kg (2lb 4oz) white sugarpaste (rolled fondant) for the drum board

1 heaped tsp gum tragacanth

Pearl white lustre

Royal icing (see page 16)

Equipment

Two 20cm (8in) thin teardrop-shaped cake boards

20cm (8in) thin heart-shaped cake board

43cm (17in) oval drum board

Rolling pin

Sharp knife

Cake smoother

Closed curve serrated crimpers

Scalloped lace sheet, large lace flower, smaller lace flower moulds

Piping (decorating) bag fitted with no. 2 piping tube (nozzle)

Double-sided tape

White ribbon for cake drum board

a

1 Put each cake on the appropriate board. Cover the fruit cakes with marzipan and sugarpaste (see pages 19–20). Coat the madeira cake with a layer of buttercream and then cover with sugarpaste (see page 20). Set aside.

2 Dampen the oval drum board with a little water. Roll out the sugarpaste and cover the board (see page 20). Trim away any excess paste, then crimp around the edge of the paste. Leave to dry.

b

3 Add the gum tragacanth to 500g (1lb) of sugarpaste. Leave to stand for at least one hour before use. Dust the scalloped lace mould with pearl white dust. Roll a strip 26cm × 15mm, (10 × ½in). Press the paste into the mould and roll over it with a rolling pin. Trim any excess paste. Place the lace trim around the base of each cake with the scallops standing upwards. Fix with a little water. Think about where the joins will go as you do not want a join at the front of the cake.

4 Dust the large lace flower mould with pearl white dust. Roll out a piece of sugarpaste about 6mm (⅛in) thick. Press into the large lace flower mould then press the reverse of the mould onto the back (pic a). This will ensure the paste goes into all parts of the mould. Roll over it with a rolling pin and trim any excess paste. Make four large flowers, one for each of the teardrop cakes and two for the heart cake. Place onto the top of each cake, slightly curving the flowers to fit the shape of the cakes (refer to the photo on page 107 to help you position them). Use the same mould to make lots of tiny flowers. Just press enough paste in for a single flower. Make quite a few of these and use them for fillers and for the drum board.

5 Now use cake designs sheet 2; this has two flower designs. Make two of each flower in the same way as in step 4. Place one of the flowers at the base of the large lace flower on one teardrop cake (pic b). Fill in the odd gaps with the tiny flowers made in step 4. Repeat for the other teardrop cake, but use the second flower design. Secure in place with a little water.

6 Add the remaining two flowers at the top of the large flowers on the heart cake. Place a tiny flower in the top centre and at the point of the heart.

7 Arrange the teardrop cakes onto the drum board then place the heart in the middle, resting it on the teardrop cakes (pic c).

8 Place a few tiny flowers on the board and secure in place with royal icing (pic d). Stick double-sided tape around the drum board and trim with ribbon.

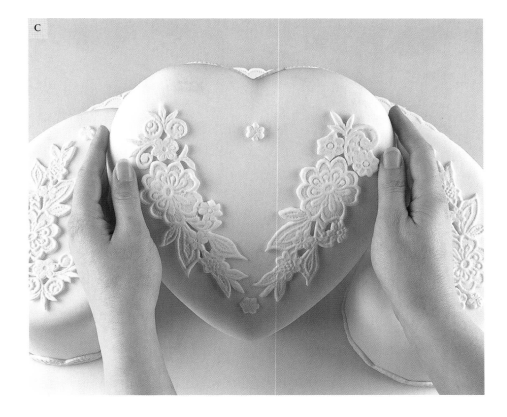

Templates

Ivory and Mint
Triangles
(pages 78–81)

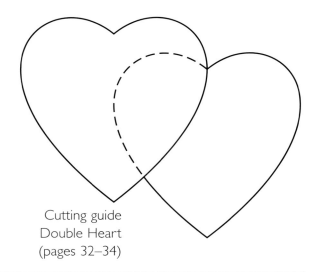

Cutting guide
Double Heart
(pages 32–34)

Below is a list of the brands of key equipment/materials used on each cake. If you cannot find the same item, simply use an alternative.

Cake smoother and piping nozzles used throughout (PME)

Enchanting Butterflies pg 26 – closed scallop serrated crimpers (PME), butterfly cutter set (Patchwork Cutters), high tubular separator (Culpitt Limited)

Chocolate Heart pg 29 – arum lily cutters (Patchwork Cutters), petal veining tool (Jem)

Double Heart pg 32 – dove on double gold ring decoration (Culpitt Limited), lily bouquets/bubble texture roller (Jem), double heart cake board (Major Johnson Ltd), ribbon cutter (FMM)

She Sells Seashells pg 35 – leaf cutters (Jem)

Baskets of Flowers pg 38 – closed vee serrated crimpers/basketweave textured roller (PME), flower holders (Wilton)

Pretty Blossom pg 42 – blossom cutter (PME), acrylic stand (Culpitt Limited)

Burgundy Rose Drape pg 46 – closed triple scallop crimpers/ribbed texture roller (PME)

Rose Leaf Cascade pg 50 – closed vee serrated crimpers/veined rose leaf plunger cutters set 3 (PME), flower former set (Wilton), leaf cutters (Kingston)

Glistening Crystals pg 58 – gem branches (Culpitt Limited)

Coronet and Cushions pg 62 – rice, scroll, bubble texture rollers (Jem), bead cutter 3/straight frill sets 1–4 and 5–8 (FMM)

Daisy, Daisy pg 66 – large daisy mould (Amaco)

Christmas Rose Collar pg 70 – closed vee serrated crimpers (PME), diamond side design/Christmas rose corner cutter (Patchwork Cutters), Christmas rose cutter (Culpitt Limited), petal veining mat (FMM)

Lace and Hydrangeas pg 74 – triple serrated crimpers (PME), small leaf cutter (Kingston), Chantilly, Austrian, lily lace cutters (Devon Ladye)

Ivory and Mint Triangles pg 78 – closed scallop serrated crimpers (PME), lace flower cutter (Jem), lace leaf set (Orchard)

White Wedding pg 82 – closed scallop serrated crimpers (PME)

Pink Bubbles pg 86 – closed curve serrated crimpers (PME)

Pretty in Pink pg 90 – closed triple scallop serrated crimpers/cutting wheel (PME), leaf scroll cutter (Jem), textured lace heart cutter set 2 (FMM)

Regal Elegance pg 94 – closed triple scallop plain crimpers/creative plaque cutters sets (PME), flower holders (Culpitt Limited), formers (Kingston)

Frills, Flowers and Pearls pg 98 – bulbous cone tool/round garrett frill cutter (PME), ribbon cutter/bead cutter (FMM), fabric texture roller/endless garrett frill cutter (Orchard)

Swags and Roses pg 102 – closed curve serrated crimpers/veined rose leaf plunger (PME), ribbon cutter (FMM)

Victoriana Flower and Lace pg 106 – closed curve serrated crimpers (PME), scalloped lace sheet, large lace flower, smaller lace flower moulds (CK Products)

Suppliers

UK

Cee for Cakes
PO Box 443
Leighton Buzzard
Bedfordshire LU7 1AJ
Tel: 01525 375237
Fax: 01525 385414
Email: info@ceeforcakes.co.uk
www.ceeforcakes.co.uk

Culpitt Ltd
Jubilee Industrial Estate
Ashington
Northumberland NE63 8UQ
Tel: 01670 814545

Devon Ladye
The Studio
Coldharbour, Uffculme
Devon EX15 3EE
Tel: 01884 841316

FMM Sugarcraft
Unit 5, Kings Park Industrial Estate
Primrose Hill, Kings Langley
Hertfordshire WD4 5T8
Tel: 01923 268699
Fax: 01923 261226
Email: sales@fmmsugarcraft.com
www.fmmsugarcraft.com

Knightsbridge PME
Knightsbridge Bakeware Centre
Chadwell Heath Lane
Romford
Essex RM6 4NP
Tel: 0208 590 5959
Email: online.orders@cakedecoration.co.uk
www.cakedecoration.co.uk

Major Johnson
105 Lakey Lane
Hall Green
Birmingham B28 9DT
Tel: 0121 778 4692

Orchard Products
51 Hallyburton Road
Hove
East Sussex BN3 7GP
Tel: 01273 419418
Fax: 01273 412512

Patchwork Cutters
123 Saughall Massie Road
Wirral
Merseyside CH49 4LA
Tel: 0151 6785053
www.patchworkcutters.com

Renshaw Scott
Sherburn-in-Elmet
Leeds LS25 6JA
Tel: 0870 870 6950
Fax: 0870 870 6951
Email: info@renshawscott.co.uk
www.renshawscott.co.uk

Squires Kitchen
Squires House
3 Waverley Lane
Farnham
Surrey GU9 8BB
Tel: 01252 711749
Fax: 01252 714714
Email: productinfo@squires-groups.co.uk
www.squires-group.co.uk

Sugarflair Colours Ltd
Tel: 01268 752891

USA/CANADA

CK Products
Tel: (+1) 260 484 2517
Fax: (+1) 260 484 2510
www.ckproducts.com

Wilton Enterprises
Tel: (+1) 630 963 1818
Fax: (+1) 630 963 7196
www.wilton.com

Wilton Industries Canada
Tel: (+1) 416 679 0790
Fax: (+1) 416 679 0798

NEW ZEALAND

Decor Cakes Ltd
Otahuhu, Auckland
Tel: (09) 276 6676

Innovations Specialty Cookware & Gifts
Birkenhead, Auckland
Tel: (09) 480 8885

Spotlight
(branches throughout New Zealand)
www.spotlightonline.co.nz

Sugarcrafts NZ Ltd
Panmure, Auckland
Tel: (09) 527 6060

AUSTRALIA

Cake Art Supplies
MIRANDA, NSW 2228
Tel: (02) 9540 3483

Cake and Icing Centre
MITCHELTON, QLD 4053
Tel: (07) 3355 3443

Petersen's Cake Decorations
OCONNOR, WA 6163
Tel: (08) 9337 9636

SOUTH AFRICA

The Baking Tin
Claremont 7700
Cape Town
Tel: (021) 671 6434
Stores also in Durban,
Bloemfontein, Skiereiland and
Randburg

Jem Cutters
Pinetown 3610
Durban
Tel: 031 701 1431
Fax: 031 701 1559

South Bakels
Paarden Eiland 7420
Cape Town
Tel: (021) 511 1381
Stores also in Johannesburg and
Bloemfontein

Index